SPORTS ASTROLOGY

SPORTS
ASTROLOGY

John Frawley

APPRENTICE BOOKS

Published 2007 by Apprentice Books
www.johnfrawley.com

ISBN 978 0953977420

Cover photograph by Sergio Bondioni, Yellow Brick Studios
Design and typesetting by John Saunders Design & Production

Contents

To the Reader

The purpose of this book is to teach you something. If you read it, you will learn a little; if you work through it, you will learn a lot. The book is cast as a dialogue between master and student. I encourage you to put yourself in the place of the student. Whenever a question is asked, try to answer it yourself before reading on. Judge the charts yourself, rather than simply reading the judgements given. That way lies knowledge.

This is not an encyclopedia of techniques. I see no purpose in presenting a multitude of methods, most of which do not work. Here are a few methods that I have tried and found do work, as I have repeatedly demonstrated on television (on my own daily show, *Frawley and the Fish; Odds on Sport; Predictions!; London Tonight; Under the Moon; Richard Littlejohn – Live and Direct*) and in print (*The Astrologer's Apprentice; FourFourTwo; Total Football; The Manchester United Magazine*). The core of the book is the system I have developed for judging the result of a sporting contest using a chart set for the start of the event. This works well, but there is room for improvement. My hope in writing this book is that someone will pick up this system and make the improvement. Onward!

I have wrestled hard with the Atlantic Ocean, without being able to defeat it. 'Manchester United *is* playing Arsenal,' as an American would write, may be grammatically correct, but sounds horribly pedantic to the English ear. English ears being the only variety I possess, I trust I shall be forgiven for sticking with 'Manchester United *are* playing Arsenal' and even 'the team *are...*'.

For simplicity, the terms 'Lord 1, Lord 2, etc.' are used here to mean 'the planet that rules the sign on the cusp of the first house, second house, etc.' If, for example, the second cusp is in Cancer, Lord 2 will be the Moon, ruler of Cancer.

Acknowledgements

So many years have passed since Olivia Barclay first encouraged me to write this book, that I fear memory may not stretch back far enough to acknowledge many whom I would wish to thank. Shining like beacons through the clouds that enwrap recognisance are Sandy and Pat Curran, with whom I have enjoyed long discussions on sports prediction – and Pat's attempts to explain American football to me. Also helping to bridge the Atlantic, Tom Callanan has poured copiously from his wealth of baseball lore in response to my every query.

Mike Edwards introduced me to John Addey's system for predicting horse-races, and I am grateful to Tim Addey for his warm support when I proposed discussing his father's work. Frank Clifford has been as generous as ever with the results of his data-collecting. Christian Borup and Patrick Casey have hunted out references for me.

Tony Baldwin, Bernhard Bergbauer, Anne Coralie, Louise Hutson, Anne Sandu, Yoko Sugimura, Tony Tsousis, and Yasha Yothi have provided charts for the book, and stimulating conversation upon them. I apologise to anyone whose name I have omitted from this list. Nina Holly, Richard Redmond, Branka Stamenkovic, and Carol Walsh scoured the manuscript, providing valuable suggestions and corrections. The errors that remain are mine alone.

I wish to thank Marybeth Beechen and Chad Henry for all the effort they exert to further understanding of the Real Astrology.

My greatest thanks must, as ever, be to the one who has borne with me through the months of gestation and a most prolonged labour. Without the patience, tolerance, and loving support of my wife, Anna, there would be no *Sports Astrology*.

Some people believe football is a matter of life and death. I'm very disappointed with that attitude. I can assure you it is much, much more important than that.

Bill Shankly

Key

♈	Aries	ruled by Mars
♉	Taurus	ruled by Venus
♊	Gemini	ruled by Mercury
♋	Cancer	ruled by the Moon
♌	Leo	ruled by the Sun
♍	Virgo	ruled by Mercury
♎	Libra	ruled by Venus
♏	Scorpio	ruled by Mars
♐	Sagittarius	ruled by Jupiter
♑	Capricorn	ruled by Saturn
♒	Aquarius	ruled by Saturn
♓	Pisces	ruled by Jupiter

♄	Saturn
♃	Jupiter
♂	Mars
☉	Sun
♀	Venus
☿	Mercury
☽	Moon

☊	North Node of the Moon
☋	South Node of the Moon
⊗	Part of Fortune/Fortuna

☌	Conjunction	same degree, same sign
☍	Opposition	same degree, opposite sign
△	Trine – 120 degrees	same degree, 4th sign round
□	Square – 90 degrees	same degree, 3rd sign round
✶	Sextile – 60 degrees	same degree, 2nd sign round
℞	Retrograde	appears to be going backwards

1

He arrives and the journey begins

I was sitting at the mouth of my cave, boiling a few roots to make the simple soup that is all the mortal sustenance a Master Astrologer either needs or desires, when a squawk from my pet raven alerted me to the impending arrival of a gaudily clad youth, whom I could see guiding his mule along the winding track that leads up the hillside. I calculated (Solar Fire 6) that I had just time enough to eat the soup before he arrived, so was applying a balm of ewe's milk to my burning tongue as he dismounted.

'Master', he began, 'your prowess in predicting sports results is the subject of unceasing wonder in every land through which I've travelled.'

'How much wonder?' I asked.

'Lots of wonder,' he replied.

'Is that all?'

'Oh, lots and lots of wonder. First magnitude wonder.'

'Ah!'

'I want to learn your secrets. Teach me, oh Master!'

'My child, do you understand that which you ask? Are you ready to abjure all interest in the fleeting pleasures of this world?'

'I am.'

'Are you ready to mortify your flesh, spending days and nights in unending toil?'

'I am.'

'Do you have a Visa or Mastercard?'

He rummaged in his saddle-bag till he found one, which I then handed to Sedna, my raven, who hopped into the cave to process the transaction. We sat in silence, small beads of nervous perspiration forming on his upper lip, until Sedna emerged, bearing a slip of paper, which he gave to the boy, and his card, which he gave to me. 'I'll hold onto this,' I explained. 'There will doubtless be other expenses along the way. Now we can begin.'

Saying this, I hit him sharply across the shoulders with the stick I had been using to poke my cooking-fire. 'Thank you, Master,' he said, bowing low.

'He will be a good student,' I thought. 'Best order more sticks.' I passed the card back to Sedna.

'Tell me, my boy,' I began, 'which sports do you wish to predict?'

'All sports, Master. I would be proficient in all, from football to crown green bowls.'

'And what do you mean by *football*?' I was testing him.

'There can be no dispute among the lovers of wisdom, Master. As the circle is the perfection of all plane figures and hence the sphere is the perfection of all solid shapes, so must the form of football known to the heathens as "soccer" be the perfection of all sport. Indeed, Josephus recounts how, not long after his banishment from Eden, Adam fashioned a football after the image of the celestial orbs to have a kick-about with Seth. It was only in recent times that Johannes Kepler, his view of heavenly things obscured by the fogs of Bohemia, modelled a still further fallen universe based upon that imperfect shape, the ellipse. While angelic beings continue to play the divine game, the denizens of darkness follow Kepler with their strange local variants using odd-shaped orbs.'

'You understand well, boy. Any astrologer must recognise the superiority of the spherical game. Despite their baser nature, however, those bizarre variants of the sport are nonetheless predictable too.'

'Golly gee, Master! Can you teach me to do that?'

'Keep that Mastercard topped up and I will teach you all I know. Now, let us begin. Sit on that stone and prepare to take notes.'

I whistled, and a yak who had been grazing peacefully beside a nearby spring ambled over. 'Stand there, Britney,' I asked her. I took a chalk from my pocket and began to write on her black flank as I began my first discourse.

I began with another test. 'Where shall we start our investigation of sports astrology?'

He gave me a look of the 'do you think I was born yesterday?' variety before answering, 'With horary, of course: the best starting point for any study of astrology'.

I smiled, but hit him with my stick, as a precaution. 'Well done, my child. But be warned. My venerable teacher told me:

STUDENT WHO ATTEMPTS TO MASTER ONE AREA OF HORARY WITHOUT MASTERING ALL IS LIKE YAK WHO BALANCES ON ONE LEG.

It is important that you have a sound knowledge of horary in all its applications.'

He leaped up and ran to his saddlebag, from where he produced a battered blue volume that looked as much used as a well-loved teddy bear. 'This book has been my study by day and my pillow by night. Deep have I drunk of its wells; fully have I feasted at its groaning table; high have I soared on its spiralling thermals; happy have I wallowed in its mud-pools....'

'Less is more, dear boy. What, pray, is it?'

'That deathless masterpiece *The Horary Textbook*, written by that fine fellow John Frawley, published by Apprentice Books and available through any good bookshop for only £22.'

'You have chosen well. Devoted study of that book should give anyone a fair grasp of horary. Now tell me, in a nutshell, what is horary.'

'It is the astrology of interrogations. The chart is cast for the time and place at which a question is asked, and, in the words of the great master of horary, William Lilly, judgement is drawn "instantly".'

'A definition close enough for most purposes. To be exact, the chart is cast for the time and place at which the astrologer understands the question. If the astrologer is working on his own question these will, of course, be the same as the time and place at which it was asked. More often than not, that is the case with sports astrology. Use Regiomontanus houses. Consider only major aspects and disregard cosmic flotsam such as Uranus, Neptune and that cartoon dog.

'But you know all that, and if you do need to refresh your memory of the basics you can turn to *The Horary Textbook*. We can concentrate on the application of horary to sport.'

'Where do we begin, Master?'

'With the questions. We can divide sporting horaries into four kinds:
>contests: *Will we win this match/this series?*
>title fights: *Will the king lose his crown?*
>long-term forecasts: *How will we fare this season?*
>beating the bookie: *Will I profit?*

Each of these categories demands a different approach to the chart. We'll wait till your education has reached chapter 4 before we look at profit charts. The other types we can consider now.'

I plucked a feather from Sedna's tail, picked up a leaf fallen from the mountain palm (*Treeus usefulus*) that flourished beside my cave, and began to write. He watched in curious silence, as if I were writing a prescription. 'Take this,' I said, as I handed him the leaf. 'Use it as a worksheet until you have memorised the method.' He studied it attentively. 'We'll start with contest questions, as these are the most common. What is our first step?'

HORARY CHECKLIST

Cast chart for time and place of a question.
Regiomontanus houses.
Seven planets only.
Major aspects only.

Select the appropriate houses.
    Check the condition of these houses.

Locate the house rulers.
    Check: are they combust, under the sunbeams, cazimi, opposing the
            Sun?
           house placement
           are they conjunct the Nodes?
           speed and direction
           aspects
           are they besieged?
           are they on Regulus, Spica or Algol?
           are they in their joy?
           essential dignity/debility
           receptions between the rulers: does one dominate the other?

If the Moon is one of the house rulers:
        how much light does it have?
        is it in the via combusta?

Select the appropriate houses

From the worksheet, he read, 'Select the appropriate houses.'
   'How do we do that?' I asked.

'In horary, the querent gets the first house.'

'Yes. But the person asking the question isn't usually involved in the match. The querent in a sports horary is usually asking about someone else's chance of victory.'

'Uh, I see the problem. But can't we take the first house for anyone the querent strongly identifies with?'

'Good! Yes, we must administer the We Test.'

'Isn't that what they use in athletics?' he giggled. I broke a stick across his head, although Sedna found his comment most amusing.

When the bird's cackling had quietened enough for me to be heard, I continued: 'We must find out if the querent supports the team that's playing. A useful way of doing this is to ask what the querent would say if the team won. Would it be *we* won, or would it be *they* won? If it is *we* won, we can give the team the 1st house. The opponents, therefore, will have the 7th, the house of open enemies.'

'And what if it is *they* won? The team he names is given the 7th house?'

'No. If the team is not *we*, we must investigate a little further. It isn't only the teams people support that they can have a strong view on. You, for example – is there some team that you hate?'

'Yes!' he exclaimed. 'Madcaster Rovers!'

'I agree. What right-thinking person, what scoundrel so deep-dyed, could support such a collection of cutthroats, villains and general no-goodniks as Madcaster Rovers?'

Emboldened by my affirmation, he stood, cupping his hands to his mouth, sending a cry of 'Madcaster, BOO!' echoing among the peaks. Even Britney raised her head to add her bellow of disapproval that so foul a name as Madcaster had sullied the pure air of this, our Shangri-la.

'There are many reasons for someone wanting to know how the team they hate will fare in a certain match. Perhaps that team is their own team's local rivals, or there is a long-standing grudge between them. Perhaps that team winning will rob their own of the championship, or condemn them to relegation, even though the two teams are not playing each other. Whatever the motive might be, the hated team is given the 7th house and its opponents the 1st.'

'Because the 1st house is the 7th from the 7th, my enemy's enemy?'

'That's right. Or maybe the querent has no personal interest in the match, but has a personal interest in someone who has. The question *Will Chelsea win?* might translate as *Will the team my son supports win?* Such cases are not so common, but when they occur we can treat them as that other person's *we*. My son's team, for instance, would be the 5th, its enemy the 7th from the 5th, which is the 11th.'

'Suppose it's not a team game. A tennis match, perhaps.'

'It's less common for an individual player to pass the We Test, but it still happens. An Aussie querent might well be supporting the Aussie player, while a British querent might support the Brit.'

'Is there any purpose in judging horaries about British tennis players?'

'Not really. Just say "No". You'll usually be right. People find likes and dislikes among sportsmen for any number of reasons. As long as the querent has a genuine partiality one way or the other, we can judge. It doesn't have to be a consuming passion: a significant preference for one over the other is enough.'

'Suppose the querent doesn't support the team, doesn't hate them, has no interest in anyone who does support them or hate them. What then?'

'Then, we might well wonder why the question is being asked. Especially if there is a consultation fee. Often, even with a team the querent supports, the real question is *Will I profit by betting on this team?* We must be quite clear about this. If the querent's interest is in a potential profit, we must address this as a profit question, not as a contest question. This is an important rule in all horary: be clear on what is being asked.

JUDGE THE WRONG QUESTION AND YOU'LL GET THE WRONG ANSWER.'

'OK. But suppose the querent isn't trying to win money.'

'Then, my boy, we have a problem. You will hear it suggested that you can give the 1st house to the home team or to the team the querent mentions, or mentions first. Such suggestions are fine – unless you want to get the right answer from the chart. If the querent is indifferent to both teams we have no grounds for assigning houses.'

'So what do we do?'

'Nothing. We can't judge the question. We may, however, be able to make a prediction from the chart for the event itself. You'll find out how to do that in chapter 2.'

'And what if it isn't a one-to-one contest? Suppose the querent is asking *Will my hero win this golf tournament?* One player against many. Is that 1st house against 7th house, too?'

'Is there no end to the boy's questions?' I wondered. 'No,' I replied. 'This is a question of one player against a field. We'll look at methods for judging this later.'[1]

---

[1] See pp. 49–62 below and chapter 3.

I thought for a peaceful moment he had run out of points to raise, till suddenly he became agitated, as if stung. 'Master, Master!' he cried in his distress, 'We've dived straight into selecting the houses. Shouldn't we have checked for *Considerations before Judgement* before doing that? The chart might not be radical. We might not be able to judge it. We might get it wrong!'

I gestured to Sedna, who flapped off into the cave to process an order for more sticks, while I composed a polite response. 'These considerations were developed to give the astrologer an excuse for not judging any chart that might jeopardise his safety. Astrology does not stop working! If it did, the merest peasant could seize one of these gaps in fate to make himself emperor, or do whatever else might please him. Have you ever heard someone say "This isn't radical. It can't be judged," when looking at a birthchart?'

'No, Master.' His agitation had disappeared.

'Regard for these considerations is the hallmark of the amateur, the dilettante. The professional – so long as he is not working for a bad-tempered king – has no need of them. You may not wish to be a professional astrologer, my boy, but you can at least learn to think like one. That is essential if you wish to reach a professional standard of judgement.'

'Yes, Master.'

'And anyway,' I continued, tapping out my words on his skull with my stick,

THERE'S NOTHING WRONG WITH BEING WRONG.

Getting things wrong is most beneficial, both in what you will learn from it and – even more important – in preventing you from flying up your own astrological backside.' Britney mooed in agreement.

He thought for a while, digesting all that I had told him. 'So, Master, we have our houses, which will usually be the 1st and the 7th.'

'Yes.'

'What about the other houses?'

'Ignore them. Horary is simple; keep it so. I have seen so many horary judgements drown in a sea of confusion as the artist tries to find the team's fans, its coach, its finances and its star player's mistress in the chart. Don't! All we want to do is find out who will win. 1st house and 7th house, that's all. You don't have to give a commentary on the match: the result alone is sufficient.'

'What about the referee? He can have a big influence on the game.'

'Is he going to score a goal or hit a home run?'

'No, Master.'

'So leave him out of it. Even if he is partial, the team must still achieve more than the other team in order to win. The losing team may blame it all on the referee, the weather, the poor quality of the pitch; we won't.'

Consider the houses

'Our first step is to look at the houses themselves to see if anything is affecting them, for better or for worse. Is there anything in either of our chosen houses? Remember that the 5 or so degrees before the house cusp are considered as being part of that house, *provided they are in the same sign as the house cusp.* If the Ascendant is at 12 Aries, a planet at 8 Aries is in the 1st house, not the 12th. If the Ascendant is at 1 Aries, a planet at 29 Pisces is not in the 1st house, but is still in the 12th.'

'This is true even if the planet is retrograde, Master?'

'Yes, even if it is retrograde. Use your common sense to decide where the boundary lies: it will be somewhere around the 5 degree mark. Now, if there is nothing in the house, we can move on. If there is something there, we must consider whether it benefits that house, harms it or has no effect.'

'Master, you said if there is nothing in the houses we can move on. But what about aspects to the house cusp? Don't they affect the house?'

'They do. But because we are looking at houses that are opposite each other, if something aspects the cusp of one it will also aspect the cusp of the other. If Saturn is square the Ascendant it is also square the Descendant. Any such planet will share its influence equally, so we can ignore it. The only aspect to a house cusp that concerns us here is conjunction, and that is covered by a planet being in a house.'

'What about opposition?'

'If we were looking at houses that weren't opposite each other, yes. But a planet conjunct the 1st cusp will oppose the 7th cusp, and vice versa. Use the conjunction and ignore the opposition.'

'So a malefic planet in the 1st house is an affliction to the good guys. A malefic planet in the 7th afflicts the bad guys.'

'Yes. But what do you mean by a malefic planet?'

'Mars or Saturn.'

'No!' I lifted his chin with the end of my stick. This point is important, so I needed his full attention. 'Any planet can be malefic. Mars and Saturn can be benefic.

ANY PLANET WITH ESSENTIAL DIGNITY IS BENEFIC
ANY PLANET IN ITS DETRIMENT OR FALL IS MALEFIC

It doesn't matter which planet it is: it is the dignity or debility that makes it either benefic or malefic. Got that?'[2]

'I think so, Master. If Venus is in Virgo, it afflicts the house it is in. If Saturn is in Aquarius, it helps the house it is in. Is that right?'

'Yes, that's it. Be careful, though: we are not discussing Lords 1 and 7 now. We are talking only about the other five planets. We'll look at Lords 1 and 7 in a minute.'

'Yes, Master. Only the other five planets.'

'Lords 6, 8, and 12 are said to be accidental malefics, because they rule these unfortunate houses. In theory, their placement in a house afflicts that house. But that is theory; in practice, we can ignore this in contest horaries. These houses aren't relevant to the matter at hand.'

'What about the Nodes, Master?'

'Their testimony in these horaries is very simple: North Node in a house helps that house; South Node in a house afflicts that house.'

'So if the North Node is in the 1st, that's good for our team. And if the South Node is also in the 7th, that afflicts our enemies, so that's doubly good news!'

'No, my boy. The Nodes are opposite each other. If the North is in the 1st, the South will always be in the 7th. This is one testimony, not two. The Nodal axis favours one team or the other.'

'And if the Nodes aren't in the 1st and 7th?'

'Then they are irrelevant, unless Lord 1 or Lord 7 is conjunct one of them. Now, here's another important rule, important in all astrology:

THE CLOSER, THE STRONGER

The closer the affecting planet is to the house cusp, the greater the affect it will have. Suppose there is a malefic planet in the 1st house, just 3 degrees away from the cusp, and there is another malefic in the 7th, 15 degrees away from the cusp. Which house is the more afflicted?'

'The 1st, Master.'

'Yes, good. Also:

---

[2] For further explanation, see my *The Horary Textbook*, p. 45; London, 2005.

SIGN BOUNDARIES ACT LIKE INSULATORS

A planet that is in a house but not in the same sign as the cusp of that house affects that house, but nowhere near as strongly as a planet that is in the house and in the same sign as the cusp. This is true no matter how close the planet is to the cusp.'

He looked uncertain. 'Give me an example, Master.'

'Suppose I cast a horary. The Ascendant is at 10 Libra and there is a benefic at 29 Libra. Then you cast a horary. The Ascendant is at 28 Scorpio and there is a benefic at 1 Sagittarius. Whose 1st house is most helped, yours or mine?'

'The benefic in my horary is much closer to the cusp. You told me *the closer, the stronger*. But on the other hand, in my horary there is a sign boundary between the cusp and the benefic. That acts like insulation. I'd say your 1st house is probably helped the most.'

'And you would be right. Even though the benefic in my chart is so much further from the cusp, it still has more effect than the benefic in yours, which is in a different sign to the house cusp. Though the benefic in yours still has an effect.'

'Does the Part of Fortune help a house?'

'No. In fact:

IGNORE ARABIAN PARTS

I've not found them to have any importance in these horaries – not even the Parts with such tempting names as the Part of Victory. The Parts play much less of a role in horary than they do in natal astrology, and in this particular application of horary they have no role at all. It is a common error to think that the presence of the Part of Fortune benefits a house. It doesn't. It's a rule: Parts don't do, they are done to. So how can the Part benefit something?'

'I see. Should I pay any attention to a Part's dispositor? I know that the dispositor of an Arabian Part signifies that thing – like the dispositor of the Part of Surgery signifies surgery.'

'That is true. But you are still better off ignoring them. If you want to be fussy, you could look at the dispositor of the Part of Fortune. Finding that tucked inside the enemy's house is a bad sign, though only a minor one. It is most unlikely to swing a judgement.'

'What about Fixed Stars?'

'These, too, you can pretty much forget. The stars become more important the higher up the astrological scale we go. Horary is close to the bottom of that scale.

Regulus within a couple of degrees of the cusp would favour that house. Antares could be a negative. Regulus is now at 29 Leo, Antares at 9 Sagittarius. You can safely ignore the others.'

'But Master, on my checklist you've written "are they on Regulus, Spica or Algol?" Now you're saying that Regulus and Antares are the only stars worth noticing.'

The lad had his wits about him. 'Regulus and Antares are the only ones that will have a significant effect upon a house in these horaries. Regulus, Spica and Algol are the only ones that will have a significant effect upon a planet. I'll tell you about that in a while.'

Locate the house rulers

'We've now considered the condition of the houses. As often as not, there's nothing happening to either of them. The next step is to locate the house rulers. How do we do that?'

'The planet that rules the sign on the cusp rules that house. So the ruler of the sign on the 1st cusp is Lord 1, and signifies the querent's team. The ruler of the sign on the 7th cusp is Lord 7, signifying the enemy.'

'Yes. There is only one significator per team, and that is the ruler of that team's house. Do *not*, on pain of being eaten alive by wild yaks, take a planet placed in that house as significator, or as cosignificator. Planets in the house affect that house for good or ill; they do not represent the things of that house. Not even if you want them to.'

'What about the Moon, Master? Is that the querent's cosignificator?'

'Unless the querent is actually playing in the game, he isn't personally involved in the question, even though we treat his team as *we*. So no, we don't give the querent the Moon as cosignificator. This is the same in horary charts on other subjects: if the question is asked about someone else, that other person isn't given the Moon. *Where is my cat?* and I get the Moon as cosignificator. *Where is my daughter's cat?* and my daughter doesn't.'

'And if the querent is playing in the game?'

'It is to be hoped he wouldn't be asking a horary about its outcome! What chance would he have of winning if that were his attitude? Even there, the Moon would have only a tiny role. We certainly wouldn't consider its strength as part of our judgement. In these charts, the spotlight is solely on our two main significators. The other planets may be hanging around at the back of the stage, but we don't pay them any attention unless they are directly interacting with our main significators or the two relevant houses. The Moon sometimes has a role as "the flow of events", but we would need to be very short of testimony for that to become important.'

Accidental dignity of the rulers

'Once we have selected our significators, we must weigh them against each other to see who will win. In contest horaries,

**ACCIDENTAL DIGNITY IS MUCH MORE IMPORTANT THAN
ESSENTIAL DIGNITY.**

As in a horary about a court case, where essential dignity shows who is in the right, which may or may not be the person who wins the case, so in a contest horary: essential dignity may show who plays better, but this may or may not be the one who wins the game.'

'I understand the basic idea of accidental dignity, Master. Are all accidental factors of equal importance in these charts?'

'No. First, check to see if either significator is **combust**. That means within eight and a half degrees of the Sun and in the same sign as the Sun.'

'So if it is within three degrees of the Sun but in a different sign it isn't combust?'

'Yes. That's why I said "*and* in the same sign". Do pay attention. After you've had a little practice you will notice combust planets as soon as you glance at the chart; you won't need to go looking for them. Combustion is the most serious debility that a planet can suffer, so if one of our significators is combust we could almost stop there: that team will lose.'

'Do we stop there, Master?'

'No. Even though it is most unlikely that the other team's significator could be in as bad a state, we still must consider it. For a second or two.'

'What if both planets are combust?'

'That is a very rare "what if?" But it is possible. In sports where the match can be drawn, both planets combust would be testimony for that. If someone has to win, remember:

* the closer the stronger. The planet closer to the Sun is the more afflicted.
* applying is worse than separating. A planet getting closer to the Sun is more afflicted than one that is separating from it.

Reception with the Sun can also be important when judging combustion. A planet combust in its own sign or exaltation is not debilitated at all. That works much like a mutual reception between the planet and the Sun. A planet combust in its own detriment or fall is – if this is possible – debilitated even more seriously than is usual with combustion. It is afflicted by a Sun which, as this negative reception shows, hates it. Bad news indeed!'

'I've heard that Mars is not affected by combustion.'

'I've heard that too. It isn't true. Mars is as much affected as any other planet. To give you a little example of this, the winner of a horse-race was shown in the chart by Mars, which was combust. The winner was *Surfeit of Sun*. If Mars were not debilitated by being combust, it would not have been suffering from a surfeit.'

'What about **under the sunbeams**?'

'Definition, please?'

'A planet that is not combust, but is within seventeen and a half degrees of the Sun.'

'That's right. Unlike combustion, the planet does not have to be in the same sign as the Sun. This is a much more minor affliction. It weakens the planet a bit, but most charts will have more important testimony than this. As with combustion, distance from the Sun, applying or separating, and reception may make a difference.'

'Suppose a planet is *sub radiis...*'

That brought him a whack with the stick. 'Don't show off, boy. "Under the sunbeams" will do. As you were saying...?'

'Suppose a planet were under the sunbeams, Master, and about to enter combustion?'

'Good question, boy. In a contest horary, the change to combustion will not be significant. The event asked about is too short-term. If the horary question is about a long-term issue, though, such as *How will my team do this season?* this change would be important. How would we judge this?'

'Your team's not doing well now, but it's about to start doing a whole lot worse.'

'Time to send out for some Kleenex, yes. The only exception to this would be in a *Will my team win anything this season?* question, where the Sun ruled the 10th house and hence signified the trophy. In this case we want the conjunction with the Sun, and if that is what we want we must overlook the combustion.'

'Else we would never be able to have a Sun conjunction?'

'Exactly. Talking of Sun conjunctions, **cazimi** is rare, but extremely important when you find it. That's a planet within seventeen and a half minutes of the Sun.'

'You mean one that will perfect a conjunction with the Sun within seventeen and a half minutes' time?'

'No. Minutes of arc, not minutes of time. A planet whose position in the chart is within seventeen and a half minutes of the Sun's. Though looking for half minutes is too fussy: call it eighteen minutes. Combustion is the most weakening thing that can happen to a planet; cazimi is the most strengthening. A planet combust will almost certainly lose; a planet cazimi will almost certainly win.'

'Next on the worksheet comes **house placement**. Tell me about that, Master.'

'Very important. More contest horaries are decided by house placement than by any other testimony. Look to see which house each significator is in. Broadly speaking, being in an angular house makes it strong; a succedent house is neutral; a cadent house makes it weak. But it's not quite as straightforward as that. First, the division into strong/neutral/weak isn't really angular/succedent/cadent. It is:

> Houses 1, 4, 7, 10: strong
> Houses 2, 3, 5, 9, 11: neutral
> Houses 6, 8, 12: weak.

Don't try to create a pecking-order of houses within each division. There is no significant gradation of strength, for example, between the 1st, 4th, 7th and 10th.

'Then, being in an angular house makes your significator strong. But not if that angular house is the house of your enemy! Being in an angle is like being in a castle. If you're in a castle, you're in a position of strength. Unless it is your enemy's castle, in which case you're in prison.'

'So Lord 1 in the 1st, 4th or 10th is very strong, but in the 7th it is very weak.'

'That's right. And Lord 7 in the 7th, 4th or 10th is very strong, but in the 1st is very weak. Capisce?'

'Yes, Master.'

'Now, I gave you two rules earlier this morning. They both apply here, too.'

THE CLOSER, THE STRONGER
SIGN BOUNDARIES ACT LIKE INSULATORS

When assessing the planet's strength by house placement, the rule "The closer the stronger" is of importance only when the significator is in an angular house – not if it is succedent or cadent. Give me an example of how it might work.'

He thought for a while, gazing hard at Britney as if she could be cajoled into supplying the answer. 'Suppose Lord 1 is in the 10th, 2 degrees from the cusp. And

Lord 7 is in the 4th, 10 degrees from the cusp. They are both strengthened; but Lord 1 is strengthened more.'

'Good. Now give me an example of how the sign boundary rule might work.'

This question was more demanding, his thinking accompanied by facial contortions that threatened to dislocate either his jaw or, if this can be done, at least one eyebrow. At last, he had an idea: 'Suppose Lord 1 is in the 7th house, 10 degrees inside the house, and in the same sign as the house cusp. Then suppose Lord 7 is in the 1st house. Only 2 degrees inside the house, but in a different sign to the cusp. Lord 1 is much more afflicted than Lord 7, even though it is further from the cusp.'

'Oh, a fine example, my boy!' I was delighted. 'Now, one final, vital point on house placement:

A PLANET ON A CUSP CONTROLS THAT HOUSE
A PLANET INSIDE THE CUSP IS CONTROLLED BY THAT HOUSE

This is of importance only when one of our main significators is in its enemy's house. Suppose the 1st cusp is at 5 Leo. If Lord 7 is at 4 Leo, it sits on that cusp. It controls the 1st house. We lose. The planet must be within 2 or 3 degrees of the cusp and in the same sign as the cusp for this to be an important testimony. But if Lord 7 is at 6 Leo it is just inside that cusp. It is controlled by that house, like a man in prison. We win.'

'That's clear enough, Master. What if the planet is retrograde?'

'Let us continue with the same example. Suppose Lord 7 at 6 Leo is retrograde. It is in the 1st house, but is applying to the cusp. This does *not* give it power over that house. It is like a man in prison banging on his cell door: bang as much as he wants, he is still in prison.

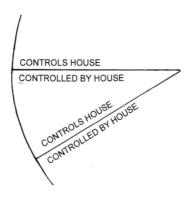

'Suppose Lord 7 at 4 Leo is retrograde. It is still sitting on the 1st cusp, but is now moving away from it. It still has power over that house, but much less than it if were direct in motion. It is like an army that has been laying siege to a castle, but is now packing up its tents and going home.

HOUSE PLACEMENT DECIDES MORE CONTEST HORARIES THAN ANY OTHER TESTIMONY

Make sure you understand it.'

With that admonition I left him to digest what he had been taught while I went to fetch Britney her lunch.

The Nodes

Britney fed, I continued. 'Conjunction with one of **the Moon's Nodes** is another factor that can decide a chart on its own. A significator conjunct the North Node is greatly strengthened; one conjunct the South Node greatly weakened. Keep to a maximum separation of about 5 degrees, with the usual rule of "the closer the stronger". In this context, it makes no difference whether the planet is applying to or separating from the Node.'

'What about aspects to the Nodes, Master?'

'There is no such thing. The Nodes neither cast nor receive aspects. We are concerned only with conjunction to them.'

'Suppose Lord 1 is conjunct the North Node and Lord 7 conjunct the South Node. Is that only one testimony, as you said about the Nodes in the houses?'

'Not at all. If one Node is in one house, the other Node will be in the opposite house. That is automatic, so is only one testimony. But our significators can be anywhere. If one of them is on one Node, there is nothing automatic about the other being on the other Node. That would be two testimonies.'

'I've noticed that the Nodes are sometimes retrograde, Master. Does that change the way we read them?'

'No, boy. Their natural direction of motion is retrograde. There is none of that sense of being against nature which is what makes retrogradation debilitating for a planet. The Nodes' direction of movement makes no difference.'

'So how strong are they, Master?'

'Very. Combustion, cazimi, and a powerful indication by house placement can all outweigh conjunction to a Node; but that in its turn will outweigh any other single accidental testimony.'

Speed and direction

'The faster a planet moves, relative to its average **speed**, the stronger it is. The exception to this is Saturn, which doesn't like going fast. It is against its nature.'

'You mean I must check the speed of all the planets in every chart? Hard work, Master!'

'No, you don't need to do that. At least, not for most sports. All you need be aware of is when a planet is approaching or leaving station. Its speed then will be slower than usual. If it is stationary, or almost so, it will be very weak. This can be an important testimony.'

'You said, "not for *most* sports"?'

'Of course, for those sports where victory is determined entirely by speed, the speed of the significators becomes much more important. If I am asking if so-and-so will win a Grand Prix, and find his significator in station, he has no chance. If he is entering a slow-cycling race he should do well. But even if speed alone decides the sporting victory, speed alone will not decide our astrological judgement: we still must consider other factors.'

'Isn't speed crucial in all sports?'

'Only tangentially. We can put a cheetah onto a tennis court. His inability to return a service means he will lose, no matter how fast he races around the court.'

'So, Master, a player whose significator is the Moon will always win, because the Moon is the fastest planet.'

I gasped, then looked long at Britney, wondering if I would not be more profitably occupied teaching her astrology. 'No, my boy. No. It is the planet's speed now, relative to its own average speed. If Jupiter is moving at 13' per day it is moving very fast, by its own standards, even though the Moon moves 13' in a matter of minutes. It is that which is important to us.' I drew a table on Britney's flank. 'You have, I'm sure, committed to memory the table of significant speeds in *The Horary Textbook*.[3] This table differs, because for our purposes here we are concerned only with extremes of speed.'

	Fast when above:	Slow when below:
The Moon	14°10' per day	12°15' per day
Mercury	1°40'	0°20'
Venus	1°10'	0°15'
Mars	0°43'	0°10'
Jupiter	0°12'	0°03'
Saturn	0°06'	0°02'

[4] p. 59

To his relief, I told him he did not need to memorise this. 'Unless you are going to concentrate on speed-based sports, you will not often need it.'

'What about **retrogradation**, Master?'

'It's worth noting, but it's not of major importance. Retrogradation will add to an accumulation of weakening testimonies, or take the shine off a strong one. It won't decide a contest on its own.'

'What if a planet is moving very fast, but retrograde?'

'In those sports where speed is important, direction is important too. Driving the wrong way round a Grand Prix circuit will not lead to victory. So this is not helpful. There may be rare occasions when speed and retrogradation can be usefully combined. If we are asking about a racing pigeon, for instance, we want to see it travelling fast back to where it was.'

'In a chart for a football match, might retrogradation show that team scoring an own goal?'

'Did someone ask you to give a commentary on the game?'

'No, Master.'

'So DON'T DO IT!'

Aspects

He looked so abashed that I quickly moved to a new subject. 'Our significators are affected by close aspects from other planets, for better or for worse.'

'So a trine from Jupiter is very helpful and a square from Saturn is a big hindrance?'

'Maybe. I see we need to discuss this in depth.

THE CONDITION OF THE ASPECTING PLANET, NOT THE NATURE OF THE ASPECT, SHOWS IF THAT ASPECT IS GOOD OR BAD

Conjunctions, trines and sextiles show things happening easily; squares and oppositions show them happening with difficulty. But even that simple division is too subtle for our purposes here. We are concerned only with what strengthens or weakens our significators. A square from a good planet will be helpful; a trine from a bad one will be weakening.'

'You're saying that it doesn't matter what sort of aspect it is?'

'Exactly. Except for an opposition, which is always an affliction. What matters is whether the aspecting planet is a nice one or a nasty one.'

'So a square from Jupiter will be good, because Jupiter is nice?'

'No. Jupiter may or may not be nice. Saturn may or may not be nice. If a planet has essential dignity it is nice. If it is peregrine or, even worse, in its detriment or fall it is nasty.'

'So an aspect from Saturn in Capricorn is nice?'

'Yes.'

'And an aspect from Jupiter in Virgo is nasty?'

'Yes.'

'So a square from Mars in Scorpio will help our significator, while a trine from Venus in Aries will harm it.'

'Exactly. The same with conjunctions: conjunction with a dignified planet is helpful; conjunction with a debilitated planet is harmful.'

'How close do the aspects need to be?'

'It's the same rule as usual: the closer, the stronger. Take 5 degrees of separation as the absolute maximum, but anything over 3 degrees will have only a mild effect. Allow a wider orb for opposition from the Sun. Being opposed to the Sun is much like being combust, so give it a maximum of 8 degrees, with anything within 4 degrees being seriously afflicted. Remember that all aspects must be within the appropriate signs. For instance, a planet at 29 Virgo opposes a planet at 28 Pisces, but not one at 0 Aries.'

'What about receptions? Do they affect the aspects?'

'Yes. Suppose your significator is the Moon, which is trined by Jupiter in Cancer. This is a nice aspect, because Jupiter is in its exaltation: it has lots of dignity. It is even nicer because Jupiter is ruled by the Moon. Or suppose your Moon is aspected by Venus in Scorpio. This is a nasty aspect, because Venus is in its detriment, and is even nastier because Venus is in the fall of the Moon.'

I could see he was trying to find a more complicated example. He found one. 'Suppose my significator, the Moon, is aspected by Mars in Taurus. What then?'

'It is aspected by a nasty Mars – in its own detriment – who likes it lots, because it is in the exaltation of the Moon. This will be significantly less harmful than an aspect from nasty Mars would otherwise have been. If it was aspected by Mars in Scorpio, the aspect is from a nice Mars (lots of dignity) who hates the Moon (in the Moon's fall). This will be significantly less beneficial than an aspect from nice Mars would otherwise have been. But still better than any aspect from nasty Mars.'

'Complicated!'

'Not really. It would be a rare chart that was decided on an aspect alone. There would have to be a terrible paucity of testimony for that to happen. So we don't need to be too subtle in our judgement of any individual aspect. It will either help a bit or harm a bit. Remember that this discussion on receptions applies only to contest horaries. Elsewhere, they become far more significant. The context here is so limiting that they work only like this.'

'What about aspects between our main significators? Are they important?'

'No. They can be ignored. In a court-case horary, an applying aspect between the significators will show the contestants settling out of court. In a sporting contest, we can assume that the opponents aren't going to kiss and make up before the game is over. If the chart were for a chess match we might take an aspect as testimony of the players agreeing a draw, but few sports offer that possibility.'

Besiegement

It was time for a practical lesson. Too much theory would addle the lad's brain. 'Stand up,' I told him, and led him to sit beside Britney. I whistled, and Sedna fluttered down to sit by his other side. They both looked at me, awaiting my signal. When I gave it, the boy cringed as Sedna pecked at him from one side while Britney snapped yakkishly at him from the other. 'Stop them, Master!' he pleaded. I did so, after a minute or two.

'How did that feel?'

'Not nice, Master.' He glared at Britney.

'That is what besiegement is like. A planet caught close between two nasty planets is besieged. Whichever way it turns, it will be harmed.' I repeated the signal. This time Britney slurped at his face with her long, warm tongue, while Sedna nuzzled him as affectionately as a raven can. The boy tried to say something, but his huge grin prevented him.

'You are now experiencing a positive besiegement. A planet caught between two nice planets is favoured whichever way it turns. This is most fortunate.' I called them off. 'As always, the closer the stronger. To be worth noting in these charts, the besieging planets should be no more than 10 degrees apart at the very most.'

'You mean nice and nasty in the same way as with aspects: dignified nice; debilitated nasty?'

'That is always the distinction, yes. A planet can also be *besieged by the rays*. If it casts its aspect into the narrow space between two nasty planets, this is weakening. If between two nice planets, it is helpful. The planets must be very close together for this to be significant in contest horaries: no more than two degrees apart at most. Even at it strongest, it is a weaker testimony than bodily besiegement.'

Fixed stars

'Fixed stars play only a small part in horary, and there are only three whose effect upon a planet is worth noting in these charts. Regulus is by far the most important of these. A significator at 28 or 29 Leo is on Regulus, and is greatly strengthened. Spica, at 23 Libra, offers some protection against defeat, but can be overruled by strong testimony. Algol, at 26 Taurus, is a negative of moderate strength. Allow a degree or so of orb either way, but no more than that.'

'You mentioned Antares before, Master.'

'So I did. But then I was talking about stars affecting a house by falling on its cusp. Now I am talking about planets being affected by falling onto a star. Different stars are worth noting in these different contexts.'

Joys

'Master, you have told me about house placement. But you didn't mention the joys of the planets. Why not?'

'I was getting to it, my boy. I didn't mention it earlier, when we discussed the strength or weakness offered by being in an angular, succedent, or cadent house, lest speaking about it then made you believe it more important than it really is.'

'So I can ignore it?'

'You're unlikely to go too far wrong if you do. But it does have some significance, so is worth noting. Each planet has one house where it is particularly happy. Being in that house strengthens it a bit. Saturn, for example, joys in the 12th. If our significator is Saturn in the 12th, it is weak, because it is cadent; but not quite so weak, because it is in its joy. The joy certainly doesn't balance out the cadency, though: it is still weak.'

'So what point is there in considering it?'

'Suppose our other significator were in the 8th house. Usually, planets in the 12th and 8th houses have about the same level of weakness. But Saturn in the 12th would be significantly less weak than a planet in the 8th. Similarly if the other significator were in the 6th. So long as that other significator wasn't Mars, which itself joys in the 6th, Saturn would have the edge.'

'Would being in its joy make Saturn in the 12th equal to a succedent planet?'

'Not in itself. But a minor affliction to that succedent planet would render them about equal. Or suppose we had Venus in its joy, in the 5th. If the other significator were angular, but afflicted in some way, maybe by an aspect, Venus' joy could render it about equal.'

'So anything else helping Venus could make it stronger.'

'Yes. A planet very close to an angle would need to be severely afflicted for Venus in joy to match it, though.'

'So overall, joys are pretty useless, Master?'

'No need to be quite so disparaging, boy. They have little effect in contest horaries because there is so little scope for subtlety here. In more complex horary questions they can be more significant. In natal work, even more so. The joys of the planets are these:

Mercury:	1st house	Moon:	3rd house
Venus:	5th house	Mars:	6th house
Sun:	9th house	Jupiter:	11th house
	Saturn:	12th house	

The Moon

'If the Moon is one of our main significators – let me stress this: I mean *only* if the Moon is one of our main significators – there are some other points we must consider: things that don't apply to any other planet, but are important when assessing the Moon's condition. First is the amount of **light** it has.'

'How do I tell that, Master?'

'The nearer the Moon is to full, the more light it has; the nearer it is to new, the less it has. For these charts, we can say that if it is more than 120 degrees from the Sun it has lots of light, so it's strong. If it is less than 60 degrees from the Sun, it has little light, so it's moderately weak. Less than 30 degrees and it's very weak.'

'Does it matter if it's **gaining or losing light?**'

'Not in these questions. If the Moon were our significator in a long-term question, though – maybe *How is my team going to do this season?* – that would be important. Moving away from the Sun shows the Moon gaining light and getting stronger; moving towards the Sun shows it losing light and getting weaker.'

'What about it directly opposing the Sun? You said that was a major affliction.'

'Good! That is as true of the Moon as of any other planet. Even though it has lots of light then, within 8 degrees of opposition to the Sun it is badly afflicted.'

'And the **via combusta?**'

'Yes, if the Moon is in the via combusta, which is between 15 Libra and 15 Scorpio, it is seriously afflicted. In most cases we would read this as a general weakening, but the connection between the via combusta and the ancient taboos around the issue of blood can give it a special significance in charts for boxing matches.'

'So if we know that the boxer signified by the Moon in the via combusta has a tendency to cut up...'

'Exactly. Now remember: these points about the Moon are relevant *only* if the Moon is one of our main significators.'

Void of course

'But what if the Moon is void of course, Master?'

'Oh, my boy, there are few things that lighten the solemn world of a Master Astrologer as much as hearing discussions of the void of course Moon. Even Britney cannot suppress a smile at the comments they contain. Nothing happens when the Moon is void, we are told. The whole of Creation stands still, holding its breath for hours or even days till the Moon moves on. So contests that start under a void Moon can have no result. Nor can those contests for which some idle astrologer casts a horary when the Moon is void. The poor sportsmen will be playing forever, getting no nearer the final whistle than Tantalus to slaking his thirst. This is, of course, utter nonsense. Life does not stop when the Moon is void.'

'So what does it mean in a contest horary?'

'If the Moon is one of the main significators, it means nothing at all. Ignore it. If the Moon is not one of the main significators, it is a minor testimony that things may not fall out as the querent wishes. That's all. It can easily be overruled.'

'The void Moon is one that makes no further aspects before leaving its present sign?'

'Yes. The Moon can be void at other times, but they need not concern us here.'

Essential dignity of the rulers

'We've dealt with the houses themselves and with the accidental dignities of their rulers. Now we must move on.'

'You mean there's more, Master? Judging one of these charts must take hours.' He looked so despondent I half expected to see tears running down his cheeks. Britney licked him again, which certainly distracted him, if it didn't noticeably cheer him up.

'No horary chart should take hours, my boy. Least of all these. Fear not: these points take far longer to explain than they do to apply. With a little practice, you'll see them all with barely more than a glance.'

Sign	Ruler	Exalt-ation	Triplicity Day	Triplicity Night	Term					Face			Detri-ment	Fall
♈	♂	☉ 19	☉	♃	♃ 6	♀ 14	☿ 21	♂ 26	♄ 30	♂ 10	☉ 20	♀ 30	♀	♄
♉	♀	☽ 3	♀	☽	♀ 8	☿ 15	♃ 22	♄ 26	♂ 30	☿ 10	☽ 20	♄ 30	♂	
♊	☿		♄	☿	☿ 7	♃ 14	♀ 21	♄ 25	♂ 30	♃ 10	♂ 20	☉ 30	♃	
♋	☽	♃ 15	♂	♂	♂ 6	♃ 13	☿ 20	♀ 27	♄ 30	♀ 10	☿ 20	☽ 30	♄	♂
♌	☉		☉	♃	♄ 6	☿ 13	♀ 19	♃ 25	♂ 30	♄ 10	♃ 20	♂ 30	♄	
♍	☿	☿ 15	♀	☽	☿ 7	♀ 13	♃ 18	♄ 24	♂ 30	☉ 10	♀ 20	☿ 30	♃	♀
♎	♀	♄ 21	♄	☿	♄ 6	♀ 11	♃ 19	☿ 24	♂ 30	☽ 10	♄ 20	♃ 30	♂	☉
♏	♂		♂	♂	♂ 6	♃ 14	♀ 21	☿ 27	♄ 30	♂ 10	☉ 20	♀ 30	♀	☽
♐	♃		☉	♃	♃ 8	♀ 14	☿ 19	♄ 25	♂ 30	☿ 10	☽ 20	♄ 30	☿	
♑	♄	♂ 28	♀	☽	♀ 6	☿ 12	♃ 19	♂ 25	♄ 30	♃ 10	♂ 20	☉ 30	☽	♃
♒	♄		♄	☿	♄ 6	☿ 12	♀ 20	♃ 25	♂ 30	♀ 10	☿ 20	☽ 30	☉	
♓	♃	♀ 27	♂	♂	♀ 8	♃ 14	☿ 20	♂ 26	♄ 30	♄ 10	♃ 20	♂ 30	☿	☿

'But even so, Master – yet more to remember.'

'What we've done so far covers the bulk of most judgements. We can look over these final points quite briefly. But look we must, for you will find charts where they are important.'

Sedna had been busy drawing the Table of Dignities on Britney's flank. 'Too much work,' I told him. 'You needn't have bothered with those minor dignities, term and face. They are of no significance in these judgements.' His expression said I might have told him that sooner, but I knew Sedna was always pleased to show he'd performed the quite unnecessary feat of memorising the whole table.

'A big discrepancy in essential dignity can tip the balance when accidental testimonies are more or less even. Suppose my significator is in its own sign while my opponent's is in its detriment or is peregrine: that would give my team an advantage. But if my opponent is accidentally much stronger, his team will still win, even if I have the advantage essentially.'

'What about exaltations, Master? Aren't they of special importance in these questions?'

'Yes. In contest charts a planet in its own exaltation is especially strong. This is the one essential factor that can be weighed against the major accidental dignities. If a planet exalts itself, what that planet signifies will be full of confidence. Confidence doesn't guarantee victory, of course, but it does make it more likely.'

'So if my planet is in its exaltation and yours is in its own sign, my planet is much stronger than yours.'

'A most unlikely circumstance, my boy, but yes, that would be so. A planet in fall is in the sign opposite to its exaltation, so that would betray a lack of confidence. Again, not a guarantee of defeat, but certainly worth noting as a negative factor.'

'What else, Master?'

'Nothing else. That's all we need know about essential dignity for judging contest horaries.'

Receptions

He looked a good deal more cheerful after that brief lesson. 'Receptions too have a limited application in contest horaries.'

'So if my planet is in a sign ruled by your planet, my team likes your team?'

That brought him a smart tap on the head. 'No, boy. Who likes whom is hardly relevant in these charts! What concerns us is who has power over whom. If your planet is in a sign ruled by my planet, your team is in my team's power. To some extent. As with essential dignity, this can tip a chart that is otherwise even, but is not usually a powerful thing in itself – except when that reception is by exaltation.'

'If my team exalts your team we think your team is wonderful.'

'That's exactly it. You think you're destined to lose. This doesn't mean that you will lose, but it does make it more likely.'

'And if my planet is ruled by your planet...'

'It will be in its own detriment. Be careful with that one. Don't count this as two separate testimonies. If Lord 1 is in a sign ruled by Lord 7, it will always be in its detriment. Or vice versa. We can ignore the reception and just say it's debilitated. Similarly if Lord 1 is just inside the 7th house (or vice versa): it is in the enemy's house. It will also be in its detriment. This is one testimony, not two.'

'What about other receptions?'

'If my planet is in the triplicity ruled by your planet, that is a minor testimony in your favour. Reception by term, face, detriment and fall can be ignored.'

'And what about mutual reception with other planets? That must be helpful.'

'No, it isn't. You're thinking in abstractions, taking a little formula: mutual reception = helpful. Don't. You must think about what these things mean. Mutual reception is like friendship: the two planets want to help each other. In a court-case horary, which has some similarities to a contest horary, that may make sense. If my planet is in mutual reception with another planet, that other planet could signify my witnesses – somebody else who is helping me. In a contest, there isn't anybody else: it's just me and the enemy. My friend may wish me well, but he isn't going to run onto the field and score a home run for me.'

'I see. There needs to be a context where the mutual reception can make sense.'

'Exactly. This is true of every testimony in every branch of astrology. No matter how glorious or how dreadful what we see in the stars, it will not happen on Earth unless there is scope for that glorious or dreadful thing within the immediate, real, context. The stars may show that I win a fortune. But if I am playing cards for matchsticks, I will not win a fortune. There is no scope for winning a fortune within the real context.

'Now – that has stuffed quite enough information into your head for one day. Go now and draw water for our evening soup. Tomorrow we can start putting this all together.'

Putting it together

Next morning we started early, beneath a glorious sky with air so clear it seemed I could reach out my hand and touch the nearby peaks. Britney settled down in her customary place, ready for another day of being a docile blackboard. Sedna was a little late in joining us. Clearly he had been in a rush, as I had to make a discreet gesture to tell him some of his breakfast was still attached to his beak. He wiped it off with a wing-tip.

'We've been through the theory. Now you'll see how that works in the hurly-burly of a chart. No account of the theory, no matter how exhaustive, can fully show how the chart is judged. Remember:

IN THEORY THERE IS NO DIFFERENCE BETWEEN THEORY AND PRACTICE. IN PRACTICE THERE IS.'

'William Lilly?'
'Yogi Berra.'

'As you gain experience, you will increasingly be able to judge charts at a glance, without going through a formal process. Until then, you must work through the points on your checklist. These points are cumulative: a planet in an angular house and on the North Node is stronger than if it were angular and not on the North Node. But we cannot reduce our judgement to an arithmetical formula. All our testimonies admit of gradation: how close to the angle? how close to the North Node? So it is impossible to fix a numerical value for any dignity or debility.'

'Will I be able to judge all charts at a glance, Master?'

'Not if you want to get the right answer, no, my boy. Well-behaved charts have clear-cut testimonies. Others do not. Many charts are finely balanced.'

'That could show a draw, couldn't it, Master?'

'Yes. That fine balance will often be testimony that the game will be drawn. If the draw is a possible outcome. If it isn't, though:

DON'T SPLIT HAIRS!

If we want reliable judgements, we must be thorough, but if the argument for each team is equally persuasive, we are unlikely to choose the victor by a microscopic analysis of testimony.'

'So what do we do?'

'First, check that we haven't missed anything. Even the most obvious of testimonies can temporarily conceal itself behind a cloud of inattention. The thing most often forgotten is antiscia.'

'An what?'

'We'll come to that. But if you've thoroughly checked everything, then checked again, and still honours are even, follow William Lilly's advice: *When the testimonies of Fortunes and Infortunes are equal, defer judgement, it's not possible to know which way the balance will turn.*[4] We don't have to provide an answer for every chart. Regard for the limitations of knowledge, whether individual or collective, is no failure.'

'But in *The Horary Textbook* it says: *always force yourself to reach a judgement.*'[5]

'So it does. Our context here is so limited, however, that this is one area of horary where we may allow ourselves to pull up short. Our choice in these charts is between black and white. If all we can see is an exact mid-grey, this is neither more black nor more white. Choosing one or the other would not be judgement,

[4] William Lilly, *Christian Astrology*, p. 123; London, 1647. The best modern edition is the Astrology Classics edition, from The Astrology Center of America, Abingdon, 2004.

[5] p. 5.

but guesswork. Mount yourself instead upon the next bejewelled camel of advice in that richly laden caravan of astrological wisdom: *save the charts so you can examine them once the outcome is known.*[6] With a sports chart, that outcome is likely to come soon, so you can quickly learn.'

'And if it is almost mid-grey, but not quite?'

'Sometimes we might detect a slight balance in favour of one team or the other. In a match that somebody must win, even that slight balance will be sufficient to show the victor. If a draw is a possible result, so is a judgement such as, "It looks like a draw, but your team might just edge it". By ruling out an enemy victory, even a hedged judgement like this has given us something.'

'Let's look at a chart.' I sketched a chart on Britney's flank. By now she had fallen asleep. '*Who will win, our guy or their guy?*'

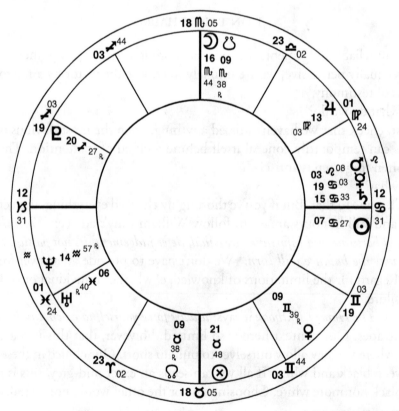

Who will win? June 28th 2004, 9.29 pm BST, 51N31 1E06.

He sat in silence, looking at me expectantly. ' No,' I told him. 'Don't wait for me to explain it to you. You must do the work. As the Ancient Masters put it, "No pain, no gain". If I explain the judgement to you, it will go in one ear and out the other. If you work at it yourself, you might remember something. So study the chart yourself and tell me what you think.'

Without hesitation he said, 'Look at the position of Lord 1! Just inside the 7th house, the house of the enemy. It looks bad for our guy.'

'So it does. So bad that we could almost base judgement on this alone. Lord 7 would have to be in a truly parlous state to be worse placed than this. But is there anything else?'

He thought for a moment. 'Lord 1 is in its detriment.'

'If placed so close to the 7th cusp, it will be. The sign on the 7th cusp is always the detriment of the Ascendant ruler. Lord 1 being in its detriment here is inevitable, so this is not a second testimony and must not be counted as such. Anyway, essential dignity makes little difference in these charts. It is accidental dignity that counts.'

He tried again. 'Lord 1 is ruled by Lord 7.'

This warranted a smack with my stick. 'If placed so close to the 7th cusp, of course Lord 1 will be ruled by Lord 7. This too is not a separate testimony. It is easy to repeat the same thing in different words and think you are piling up testimonies. This is a trap. You are not. So far we have only one testimony.'

'I know! Saturn is combust.'

'Yes, good! It is at the outer limits of combustion, but with the Sun applying to it is rapidly becoming more deeply combust. We now have two serious afflictions to Lord 1, each of which on its own would spell almost certain defeat. It is hard to imagine Lord 7 being in a worse condition, but we should glance at it, just in case.'

'It's in its fall.'

'So what? It is accidental dignity that counts in contest horaries.'

'It's right on the MC. What a powerful placement! The other guy must win.'

'And so it proved. We have two serious afflictions to Lord 1, while Lord 7 is strong. It is close to the South Node, but not close enough for this to be significant.'

'How close would it need to be for that to be taken into account?'

'5 degrees at most. 3 or less for it to be a major testimony.'

I rubbed the chart from Britney's coat and drew another. This brought some subdued snorting, as if she were arguing with someone in her sleep. 'Now compare this one. Same question: *Our guys or their guys?*'

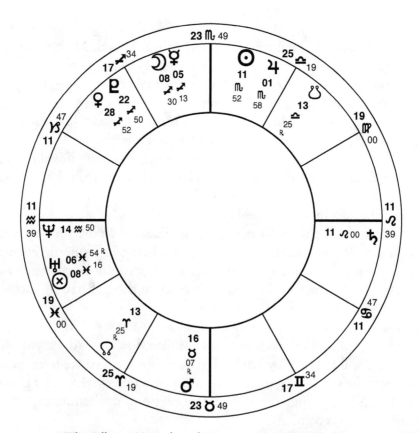

Who will win? November 4th 2005, 12.55 pm CCT, Hong Kong.

'Lord 1 on the 7th cusp: our guys lose!'

'No. Right testimony; wrong conclusion. Think again. How does this place-ment of Lord 1 differ from the one we've just looked at?'

'Here, Saturn is sitting on the 7th cusp; there, Saturn was inside it.'

'So?'

'Oh! Sitting on the cusp, the planet controls the house. Our guys control their guys. We win.'

'Exactly. *Inside* the cusp, the house controls the planet. *On* the cusp, the planet controls the house. This is so powerful a testimony it is almost conclusive. Is there anything else of note?'

'Lord 7 doesn't seem to tell us much.'

'No, it doesn't. It's in the 9th house, which is neither good nor bad. It has some minor dignity by being in its joy, but this is trivial compared to the powerful placement of Lord 1. Nothing much to be said about Lord 7; strong testimony for Lord 1. Our guys will win.'

'What about Lord 7 applying to oppose Mars, which rules it?'

'Good question, my boy. If this were about a contest taking place over a longer period, such as the World Series, America's Cup, a chess championship, or even a test match, this would be an important testimony. For a short, one-off game such as a football or rugby match, it is too distant to be counted. If it were within a degree or two it would be significant here.'

'And what about the square between the Sun and Saturn?'

'Irrelevant! Even if it were tightly applying it would have no relevance at all. An aspect brings the two things together. In this case it brings our guys and their guys together. But we *know* that's going to happen: we wouldn't have a contest otherwise. We don't need to prove that both teams turn up. Nor is it any more of a contest if we have an aspect, or any less of one if we don't. You have probably read horary judgements where an aspect is accorded great significance. If that were true, this separating aspect would show that the teams have already been in contact. The match must be over. Which was not, of course, the case when the question was asked.'

'This is so simple! We can see the judgement here at a glance.'

'This is true. We have a clear, powerful testimony in favour of one team. That's not quite enough for judgement: we must still take a quick look around the chart to make sure there is nothing equally powerful in favour of the other team. But with practice, my boy, you'll be judging charts like this in a matter of seconds.' He seemed suitably impressed. Horary is a marvellous tool.

'You must realise, though, that I am letting you in gently.' He rubbed his shoulder and looked unconvinced. 'Not all charts are quite so straightforward. This one is a little more complex. Same question: *Will we win?*' Britney rolled over in her sleep. I brushed the dust off her other flank and drew a new chart. He gazed at it thoughtfully.

'I see what you mean,' he said. 'This one doesn't seem to have a strong, clear-cut testimony.'

'So start at the beginning and let's see what we can find. Lord 1 is Mercury. How is Mercury?'

'It's in the 7th house. But it's such a long way from the cusp. And, even more, it's in a different sign to the cusp. This testimony's not so strong.'

'Oh, my beamish boy!' I chortled, 'Quite right, quite right. It's almost 14 degrees

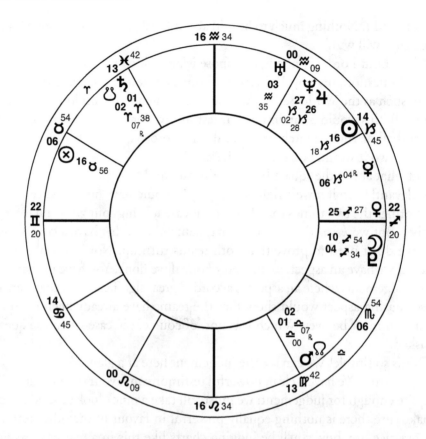

Who will win? January 6th 1997, 2.12 pm GMT, London.

from the cusp, which greatly diminishes the negative effects of its being in the enemy's house. While being in a different sign is like having a layer of protective insulation around it. This is still a minor negative testimony for the good guys, but it's nothing to get excited about. What else?'

'It's retrograde and under the sunbeams. Those are both weakening.'

'Yes, and look how far it is from the Sun. It must be turning direct sometime soon. That means it must be moving slowly and losing speed. We can check that in the ephemeris.' I tweaked Sedna's tail.

'Slow in motion,' he squawked.

'So Lord 1 is weak. That's a bad sign for the good guys.'

'What about the squares from Mars and Saturn?'

'Two debilitated malefics. Those squares would be very nasty, but at almost 5 degrees of separation, they are too distant to have any significant effect. Look now at Lord 7. How is Jupiter?'

'In its fall. But,' he added hurriedly, leaning back out of stick range, 'you've told me, Master, that essential dignity doesn't mean much in these charts.'

'Yes, accidental dignity is much more important.'

'Accidentally, Jupiter is in the 8th. That's not good. And it is under the sun-beams. Oh look, it's nearly combust!'

'It's still 10 degrees from the Sun. Again, this is something that would be impor-tant in a question about a long-term event, like a World Series. There, it would show the enemy losing power as the series progressed. It would need to be on the very point of entering combustion for us to take that into account with a short-term question like this. But, yes, it is weakened by being in the 8th and under the sunbeams. So far, there's not much to choose between them.'

'Master,' he ventured, in a voice close to silence, 'Jupiter is only half a degree from Neptune.' Britney bellowed in her sleep, outraged, and Sedna hid his head under his wing. The lad cowered, fearing my wrath for daring to mention that would-be planet. But I answered softly, 'It's so close. In many questions that would be worth noting, as an indication of some deceit or delusion. I can't see that it can carry a meaning here that would be sufficient to affect the result of the match.' Sedna brought out his head again, looking surprised and a touch disappointed.

He continued to pore over the chart. I trust, gentle reader, that you are doing the same. 'Lord 10's in a mess,' he said, at last. 'Is that a bad referee?'

'Lord 10 is certainly in a mess: in its fall, closely conjunct the South Node and opposed by a debilitated Mars. If this were a court-case horary, where Lord 10 sig-nifies the judge, this judge would be as bad as bad can be. We do best, though, to keep the referee out of contest horaries. Even if the referee is incompetent or partial, it is still the two contestants who fight it out. Lord 10 may yet have a role here, as ruler of the good guys' house of success. It's a minor role, though.'

'So Lord 4 would be ruler of the enemy's house of success?'

'It can be. But again, it's minor stuff. Such minor testimonies are most unlikely to swing a judgement. Have you noticed that Lord 4 is exactly midway between Mercury and Jupiter?'

'What does that mean?'

'Nothing of major significance. Lord 4 can show "the end of the matter" so this might suggest the result is finely poised. A close game. This could be supporting testimony for a draw. But supporting testimony only. Always take the main lines of the judgement from the main significators.'

'What about Venus? A benefic just inside the 7th house must favour the enemy.'

'At 25 Sagittarius, Venus is peregrine. It's essentially weak, so it isn't that benefic. Another minor testimony. Venus is the dispositor of Fortuna, though. Placed where it is, it is in the hands of the enemy. That's another testimony in their favour, though again, only a minor one. So far it looks finely balanced.'

'A draw, then?'

'The main significators are about equal. It would be too precious of us to try to determine which is the stronger. So a draw is likely. If this were a knock-out match, a game one team had to win, those minor testimonies would become important. As a draw is no longer possible, we can scrape the bottom of the testimonial barrel in an attempt to find something on which to hang a judgement. But you've missed something. The major testimony that makes judgement certain.'

'What? We've looked at everything.'

'No, my boy. Look again. Look at Lord 1 and the 7th cusp.' I lay back to rest my eyes. This could take some time.

I was awakened by Britney clambering to her feet. It was growing dark, time for her milking. He was still sitting by her side, despondent. 'Come,' I said, my hand on his shoulder. We walked back to the cave in silence, the sound of our footsteps echoing among the mountains, so quiet it was. I gestured to Britney to be patient a moment longer and led him to the back of the cave, where a hutch held a number of small mammals. He was entranced. 'Oh, what are they, Master? They're so sweet. Chipmunks? Some kind of marsupial? Potteroos?'

'None of those, my boy. They are antiscia. Every astrologer should have some of these little animals.' I picked one up and gave it to him. He petted it, hugging it and stroking its head. 'Take it outside and put it into that chart.'

He went back to where Britney was waiting and held the antiscion against the chart, which was still dimly visible on her coat. 'Master! Master! I see!' He was as excited as a young boy with his first puppy. 'Mercury is at 6.04 Capricorn. Its antiscion is at 23.56 Sagittarius.[7] Immediately inside the 7th cusp! Lord 1 is completely in the power of the enemy. The good guys must lose.'

'And so they did. This is the one powerful, determining testimony in this chart. It is quite as powerful as Lord 1 being there bodily, as you saw in the first chart we judged. You see, these little creatures are important. Look after the one I've given you. If you had not used an antiscion, what would you have been?'

'Wrong, Master.'

'Louder.'

[7] If you don't know how to calculate antiscia, see Appendix 1.

'WRONG, Master.'

'So don't forget this lesson. Now go feed your antiscion, while I milk Britney. That's enough astrology for today.'

We started again early the next morning. Having enjoyed a hearty breakfast, Britney was more than obliging, lying down to snooze as I made use of her pitch-black coat. 'The querent here was Norwegian. The question, *Will Norway beat Brazil?*'

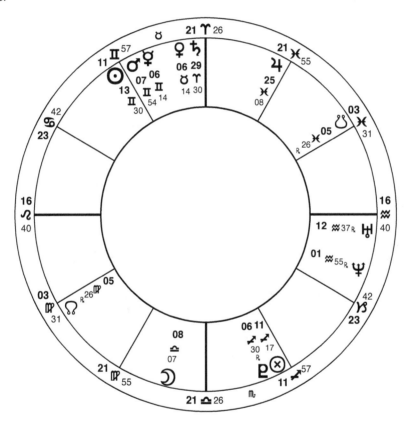

Will Norway beat Brazil? June 4th 1998, 9.46 am CED, Oslo.

'That's easy!' he said after only a glance at the chart. I invited him to explain. 'The querent is Norwegian, so his favourites, Norway, will be shown by the 1st house and their enemies by the 7th. Lord 1 is in a succedent house. Lord 7 is in an angle, very close to the MC. The enemy must win.'

'Do you have any more thoughts on this chart?'

'No. It's quite straightforward.' He sat back looking pleased with himself. That smug feeling should have been a warning to him. Rhythmic strokes of my stick reinforced my words:

'Only the Master is allowed to be smart here! Look at the receptions. What do they tell you?'

Chastened, he turned back to the chart. 'There's a mutual reception between the Sun and Saturn. The Sun is in the triplicity of Saturn. Saturn is in the exaltation and triplicity of the Sun.'

'So?'

'So the Sun has a lot more power over Saturn than Saturn has over the Sun.'

'Quite right. Especially because of the exaltation.'

'I know, Master. Let me tell you.' He was all enthusiasm again, eager to redeem himself in my eyes. 'In contest horaries, exaltation is by far the strongest of all dignities. Therefore, it is by far the strongest of all receptions too. Stronger even than sign rulership.'

'Yes, that's right.'

'So Saturn being in the exaltation of the Sun gives the Sun tremendous power over it. Sufficient to overcome the house placements. Norway win.'[8]

'And so they did. Much to everyone's surprise.'

He gazed at the chart, apparently contemplating the wonderful capacity of horary astrology. 'Master,' he asked, 'I see there's a translation of light here. Is that significant?'

'Well spotted, my boy. Yes, the Moon is separating from a trine to Mars and applies to trine the Sun. So the Moon translates the light of Mars to the Sun. Mars is Lord 10, so I see what you're thinking: perhaps we can take the 10th as the house of success. That is indeed what I thought when I judged this chart. I now incline not to do that. I think it's better to limit ourselves to the 1st and 7th houses in these horaries. You may be right, though. But be very cautious when using the 10th like that.'

'And isn't the Moon trine the Sun generally a positive testimony?'

'All things being equal, yes. It's only of secondary significance in contest charts. It becomes more important in charts where we are trying to quantify a result, rather than decide between A and B. If the question had been "Will I profit by opening this shop?" the Sun/Moon trine would have been worth noting. Here it is trivial.'

[8] This, perhaps the most surprising result of the 1998 World Cup, was predicted on TV before the tournament began.

'Are you ready for another?'

'Always, Master.'

'Same question: *Will we win?* This one is about a test match.[9] In most of the charts we've looked at, a draw was a possible result, but the charts have clearly shown victory. In test matches, the draw is a very likely result. Remember this when you judge the chart.'

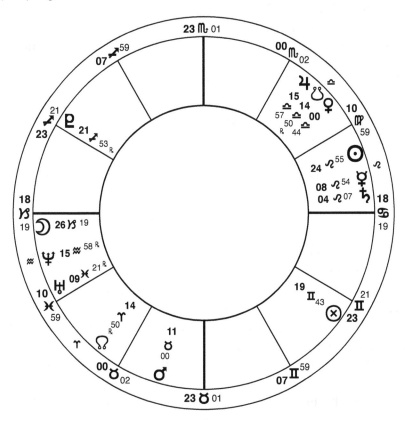

Will we win? August 17th 2005, 6.48 pm BST, Bristol.

'Oh, Master, there is a clear testimony here, too. Lord 7 just inside the 1st house.' He tried to move out of stick range without my noticing.

'Yes, good.'

'And it's in its detriment.'

---

[9] Test matches are played between only the major cricketing countries and take place over, usually, 5 days, in contrast to one-day internationals, which are regarded as less important.

'No. I mean, yes, of course it is in its detriment. But if Lord 7 is just inside the 1st house, or vice versa, it will be in its detriment. This is automatic. Because it is automatic, this is one testimony, not two. As I've told you, be careful not to think you are piling up testimonies when in fact you are merely repeating the same testimony in different words. Anyway, essential dignity doesn't much concern us in these charts. Accidental dignity and receptions. Let me repeat: ACCIDENTAL DIGNITY AND RECEPTIONS.'

'Got it, Master. Oh, look: Lord 1 is in the 7th.'

'Yes. But what is the difference between its placement in the 7th and Lord 7's placement in the 1st?'

He thought for a moment. And so, dear reader, should you.

'Saturn is in the 7th, but it's not in the same sign as the 7th cusp.'

'Yes, my boy! Well done!' I could have leaned forward and kissed him on his forehead. But that would not be befitting a Master of Astrology. 'Yes, even though it is in the 7th house, it is not in the sign of that cusp. So it is to a great extent insulated from the effects of being in that house. Better it were not there, but compared to the position of Lord 7 in the 1st, this is minor. Had Lord 7 been in another house, this would then have become significant. But even so, it is not that powerful a testimony.'

'And it's in its detriment.' His expression showed he knew he risked another beating. He did not receive one.

'Yes, this time you are right. Because it is not in the same sign as the 7th cusp, Lord 1 is not automatically in its detriment here. Do you follow this?'

'Yes, Master. Planets are in detriment when in the signs opposite the ones they rule. The sign on the 7th cusp by definition opposes that on the 1st. So the ruler of the 1st will automatically be in its detriment when in the sign of the 7th cusp. So detriment there isn't significant in these charts. But being in detriment in some other sign is significant, and here Lord 1 is in its detriment in some other sign.'

'But,' I continued, 'essential dignity is of negligible importance in these charts. What did I just tell you?'

'ACCIDENTAL DIGNITY AND RECEPTIONS.'

'So, is there anything else of significance in this chart?'

'No, Master. The querent's team must win.'

'And so it proved. The match was close, though, as might be expected from the position of Lord 1.'

'Not close enough for a draw?'

'No. We have no other important testimony here. The difference between a planet in a house while in the sign of the house cusp, and in that house while in another sign is huge. Not only in contest horaries: in any astrological chart. A planet that is in that house but in a different sign to the cusp is much less affected by its placement there, and it affects that house much less.'

'So you mean that the Sun in the 7th in this chart doesn't benefit the enemy?'

'Only trivially. Any planet in major essential dignity is benefic. The Sun is in its own sign...'

'And its own triplicity,' he chipped in.

'Yes. But beside sign rulership, that is trivial. It is in its own sign, so it is strong. How much stronger can a planet get? And this essentially strong planet is in the 7th house, which benefits that house. But...' He interrupted me again. The boy has worse manners than Britney. But he's enthusiastic.

'It's not in the same sign as the house cusp.'

'Good! You take my point exactly. Look how far it is from the house cusp. Even at 26 or 27 degrees in the same sign, the effect would wane. In another sign – no, only if there were no other significant testimonies would this be important.'

'Let's do another. This question was asked about the Oxford/Cambridge boat race. The querent supported Oxford.'

'The querent favours Oxford,' he began, 'so Oxford are signified by Lord 1, which is Jupiter. Cambridge are shown by Lord 7, Mercury.'

'Yes. What do you see?'

'Mercury's in a better house – the 10th. Jupiter is in the 11th. That gives Cambridge an advantage.'

'Yes. Even though Jupiter is also in its joy, Mercury is better placed. And?'

'The first house is afflicted by the South Node and Saturn in fall.'

'But not so much, because they aren't in the same sign as the cusp. What about the 7th house?'

'Hmm. That has a debilitated Mars in it, so that's afflicted too, though the North Node is a positive. But they're not in the sign of the cusp either.'

'No, they're not. If this were all the testimony we had, we could see that the 7th is less afflicted than the 1st. But it will be a skinny chart where this is all the testimony we have. Look back at the main significators.'

'Oh, Master, Jupiter's combust! Oxford can't win.'

'And what about Mercury? There's another strong testimony there.'

He scratched his head, his chin, his elbow, finally deciding, 'It's tightly squared by Mars and Saturn. That's not good.'

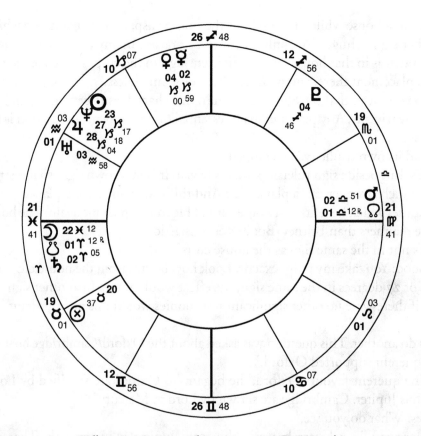

Will we win? January 13th 1997, 10.15 am GMT, London.

'That is indeed not good, though it pales into insignificance beside the combustion. But it's not what I'm looking for.'

He resumed his scratching, until a mew from inside the cave inspired him. 'Little animals! Master, the antiscion of Mercury is at 27.01 Sagittarius, right on the Midheaven. That puts Mercury in a very powerful position. What with that and the combustion, Cambridge must win.'

'And so it proved, my boy.'

'Here's another. This is another football match: *Will we win?*'

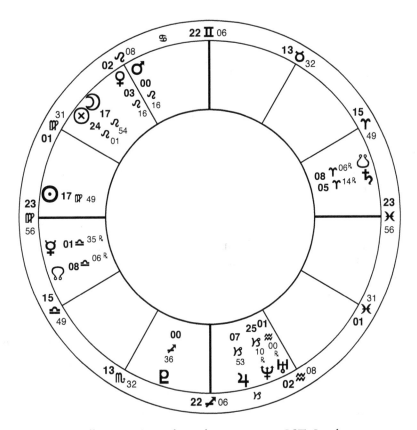

Will we win? September 10th 1996, 7.08 am BST, London.

'The querent's favourites are shown by Mercury, Lord of the 1st. The enemy is Jupiter, Lord 7. Look! Horrible stuff happening to the 7th house: Saturn and the South Node are there.'

'Yes. What about Mercury and Jupiter?'

'They're both in angular houses. But neither is in the sign of the cusp, so they're both strong, but not that strong. Mercury is about to go back into its own sign. That must be important.'

'Not here, my boy. If this had been a long-term question, maybe. But for a short-term issue, like the outcome of one game, we cannot cross the sign boundary.'

'OK. So it's retrograde: that's weakening. And it's opposed by this nasty Saturn.'

'But that's almost 4 degrees away: too far to be of great importance. Saturn afflicts Jupiter too, and more closely.'

'Then Mercury is aspected by peregrine Mars and peregrine Venus. That must count as an affliction.'

'Good. Not such a great affliction, but certainly worth noting.'

'That's about it, Master. Mercury's peregrine; Jupiter in its fall. No receptions between them. It's all much of a muchness.'

'Yes, from what we've seen so far it would be too precious to try to split them apart.'

'So was it a draw?'

'That would be the obvious answer – and would often be correct. But someone had to win this game. And anyway, you're missing something.'

He thought for a moment, then, 'It's those little animals again, isn't it, Master? Look, the antiscion of Jupiter is at 22.07 Sagittarius, exactly on the IC.'

'Well spotted! Yes, by its bodily placement Jupiter is in an angle, but not so strong because it's not in the same sign as the cusp. But by antiscion it is exactly on that angle: very powerful. There are two more testimonies here, both by antiscion. Which are...?'

'Oh look, Saturn and the South Node afflict the 7th house bodily, but not so much because they're not in the same sign as the cusp. But by antiscion they fall right on the Ascendant. That's bad news for the good guys.'

'Yes. And the third testimony?'

'By antiscion, the North Node falls right on the 7th cusp.'

He had been doing so well, it was almost a sorrow to beat him. But it was my duty. 'Foolish boy! The Nodes are opposite each other. If one is on the Ascendant the other will always be on the Descendant. That isn't two testimonies; it is saying the same testimony twice. Now, where is that final testimony?'

He stared at the chart in desperation, calculating anstiscia for everything he could see, till at last he stumbled upon the right one. 'It's Mercury, isn't it, Master? By antiscion it's just inside the 7th house, in the hands of the enemy.'

'Good! I hope you see why I set you this chart. It illustrates two very important points. First, that you cannot ignore antiscia. Here, no antiscia: no judgement. Second, it shows the difference between being in an angle in the sign of the cusp and being in an angle in a different sign to the cusp. Will you remember this?'

'Yes, Master,' he promised, rubbing his head.

Title Fights

'Now, let's consider some other types of question. Suppose we are asked *Will the champions win?* As always in horary, we must be careful with the question asked. Just because the question is phrased in such a way, it doesn't necessarily mean such a thing. *Will the champions win?* is rarely the true question, because in most sports there is no reigning champion. The team that won the Super Bowl or the Premier League, the guy who won the French Open or the Formula 1 championship: they happen to be the ones who won it last year. Within the bounds of this year's competition, they are not champions. The situation is different with boxing and some other martial arts, and also sometimes with chess. In these, one fighter is the champion, and will continue to be so until he is defeated, retires, or is stripped of his title.'

'So he's not just the guy who happened to win last year. I see. He's the one who *has* the title, not the one who *had* the title.'

'Exactly. The boxing title fight is a battle for a title that the champion currently holds. What we're really asking is *Will the king be dethroned?* Compare this with the situation in American politics. A presidential election when there is an incumbent president is like a title fight: a challenger seeks to unseat the holder, the present champ. In elections where there is no incumbent president, the battle is a straight fight between two challengers, which is the situation in most sports matches. The only time I can think of a title-fight situation in team sports was in the early years of the FA Cup. Last year's winners would be given a bye all the way to this year's final, so this year's competition was to decide who would challenge last year's champs. But that was before even my time, my boy.'

'So if we're talking about champions, I suppose the 10th house must be involved.'

'Yes, the champion will be given the 10th house, the house of kings. The challenger will have the 4th, because it is the 7th from the 10th: the house of the king's enemy.'

'But suppose the querent really likes the challenger?'

'If the querent is that ardent a fan, the challenger would be given the 1st. The champ would still have the 10th. In this case, the question is *Will we dethrone the king?*'

'And what if the querent is a big fan of the champ?'

'Then the question will be *Will we see off this challenger?* We – the champ – would then be 1st and the challenger, our enemy, 7th. If they're not already in play as house rulers, we must also consider the natural rulers:

SUN FOR THE CHAMP – MOON FOR THE CHALLENGER

The Sun being the natural ruler of kings, the Moon being natural ruler of the common people.'

'And then I judge the chart in the usual way?'

'Pretty much so. There are three important variations, though:

* A major change of dignity can show the outcome on its own. If the significator of the champion is about to enter the sign of its fall, or that of the challenger its exaltation, we have a clear testimony of victory for one or the other.

* The Arabian Part of Resignation and Dismissal (Saturn + Jupiter – Sun[10]) is worth noting. It does not reverse by night. If the champ's significator makes an immediate conjunction or opposition to this Part, it's testimony of defeat. But be cautious: you must have other testimony to back this up, otherwise he might win the fight and then announce his retirement.

* A void of course Moon can be ignored in most contest charts, because we know that something will happen: there will be a match, which will have an outcome. But in a title fight, it's a strong testimony that the status quo will be preserved. Nothing will change, so the champion will retain his crown.'

'Master, you mentioned presidential elections. Can I judge those in the same way?'

'Keep your eye on the ball, my boy! Let's not wander off. But no, you can't. They are elections, not fights, so the Moon has a determining role. It is significator of the electorate, so an aspect from the Moon to one or other contender, regardless of receptions, will overcome just about any other testimony: that contender will win. The same is true of sports that are decided by vote, such as ice-dancing.'

'Can we look at a chart, Master?'

'Of course.' I beamed at his enthusiasm. 'This horary is about a WBA Lightweight Title fight. Takanori Hatakeyama was defending his title against Julien Lorcy. What do you see?'

'The champion, Hatakeyama, is shown by the 10th house and its ruler, Mercury. The challenger is shown by Lord 4, Jupiter. Mercury is very strong, just inside its own house. Jupiter is very weak, just inside the champ's house. The favourite must win!'

---

[10] If you don't know how to calculate Arabian Parts, see Appendix 2.

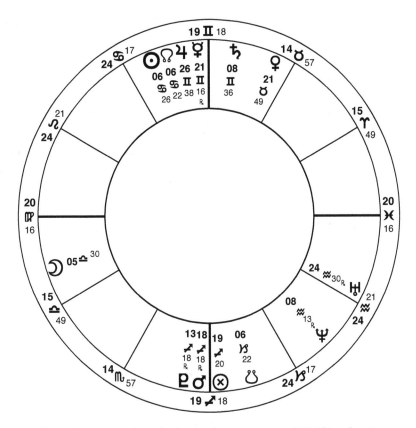

Will the champ retain his title? June 28th 2001, 10.35 am JST, Shizuoka, Japan.

My stick had lain unused too long. It fell fast and hard upon the back of his head. 'So far, yes, the testimony looks impressive. But keep looking.'

'Yes, Master. The Sun is on the North Node. That must be good for the champion, too.'

'Yes, it is. But keep looking.'

'Mercury is retrograde. I suppose that might weigh against the champ. But it doesn't seem very important.'

'Nor is it. But look how far Mercury is behind the Sun. What does that tell you?'

'Ah, it must be turning direct sometime soon.'

'Oh, very good! Yes, Mercury is in station. This is a serious debility. How can someone win a sporting contest when he's stationary?'

'Yes, Master. Now, the Part of Fortune is in the 4th house.'

'Not relevant. Fortuna doesn't make a house stronger. There is still one significator you haven't considered.'

'The Moon. Oh, it's applying immediately to the Sun – and look at the reception! The Sun is ruled by the Moon, while the Moon takes the Sun into its fall. That can't be good for the champ. Is this enough to defeat him?'

'Yes. As you've shown, Hatakeyama had strong testimonies in his favour. It was a close contest. But Lorcy won on points: the champ was defeated.'

'But surely in any horary asked at that time of year, between around June 21st and July 22nd, the Sun will be ruled by the Moon, which argues against the champ.'

'Yes. Its being ruled by the Moon isn't significant. The reception makes it more important – the fact that the Moon has power over it and takes it into its fall. But even that isn't of major significance. It is the immediate aspect that emphasises this reception, making this a major testimony.'

'Does it matter what aspect it is?'

'You can have some other kind of aspect between Cancer and Libra?'

'No, Master.'

'Well, then. Here's another. Same question: *Will the champion retain his crown?*'

'The Sun's ruled by the Moon again, Master.'

'But what did I tell you?'

'There's an aspect between them.'

'But it's separating: it's not significant. Nor is there the dreadful reception we've just seen. But in your haste, you've missed an even more important point. What does the Sun signify here?'

'It's Lord 4, Master. It signifies the challenger. We can't use it as natural significator of the champion.'

'Good. What else do we have?'

'Lord 10 is Saturn. Right on the 4th cusp: powerful testimony for the champ. It's ruled by Lord 4, though.'

'As it will be if it's on the 4th cusp. Ignore this. It is the placement that is important.'

'And it's under the sunbeams.'

'True. But that's only a minor testimony compared to that powerful placement. Had Saturn been combust, that would have been a very strong testimony. All the more so because the Sun signifies the enemy here.'

'The Moon is angular. That must favour the challenger.'

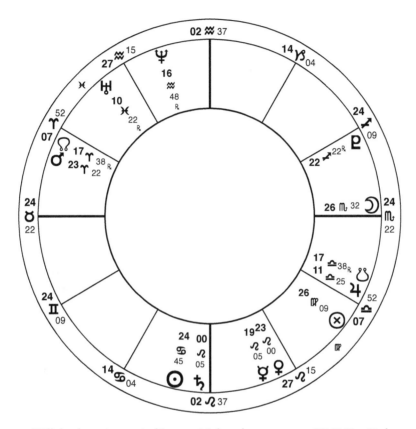

Will the champion retain his crown? July 17th 2005, 1.35 am EDT, New York.

'Yes, though it's not as strong a testimony as Lord 10 on the 4th cusp.'

'I can't see anything else, Master. The champ must retain his crown.'

'And so it proved. This querent was asking if Ronnie Coleman would retain his Mr Olympia bodybuilding title.'

'That was simple enough, Master.'

'Yes. Now, as we're talking about bodybuilders, let's digress for a moment to look at a horary about an election. The question was *Will Arnie be elected as governor?*'

'Where do I start, Master? I need to know what the querent thought about Schwarzenegger. Was she a partisan? Was she an enemy?'

'Good! Yes, we need that information to decide which house he is given. She was indifferent to him, asking just out of curiosity about this novel situation.'

'So he will be given the 7th, the house of "any old person". He is signified by

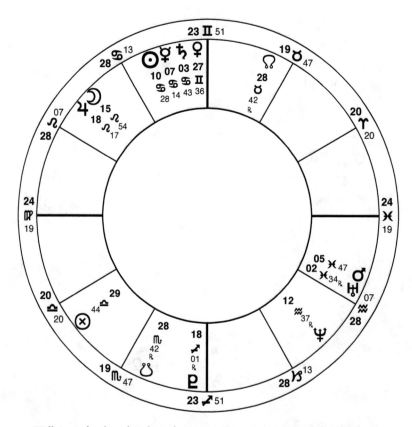

Will Arnie be elected? July 2nd 2003, 11.40 am PDT, Escondido, California.

Jupiter. The Moon goes straight to Jupiter. He will win?'

'Yes, he will win. That would be so regardless of the receptions involved. I've seen charts where the Moon is in the fall of one significator and exalts the other, but its application to that first significator gave that person the victory.'

'I suppose Mercury being combust doesn't help.'

'Quite right. Mercury rules the 1st, which is the 7th from the 7th: Schwarzenegger's enemies. They don't stand a chance. Mercury also exalts Jupiter, though this matters less in an election, where victory is decided by others, than it would do in a straight contest.'

I could see something was troubling him. Eventually he found words for it: 'You said the querent was indifferent to Schwarzenegger. How can she ask a valid horary, then? You said it isn't possible to judge the chart if the querent is indifferent to the outcome of the contest.'

'The situation here is rather different, is it not? This is not a case of Who-cares United playing So-what Town. The unusual circumstances make it perfectly reasonable that the querent should have a curiosity about Schwarzenegger's prospects, without needing to have a preference for him winning or losing. Even though she doesn't care which of them wins, Schwarzenegger and his main opponent are not on a level playing-field regarding the level of interest she has in them. Similarly, suppose Tony Blair were to give up politics and find himself contesting the Wimbledon final. Even if we don't care if he wins or loses, we could cast a judgeable horary, because we could have a higher level of interest in his fate than in that of his opponent.'

Long-term forecasts

'Now let's turn our attention away from single contests to look at a team's fortunes over a longer period. Look at this chart. The querent supported Charlton, a team used to struggling in the lower reaches of the division. This season they had reached an unexpectedly high position. The question, asked about a month before the season ended, was whether they would climb still higher. Where do we start?'

'We must find the team's significator. The querent supports the team, so it is a 1st-house question. Charlton are signified by Lord 1, which is the Sun.'

'How is their elevated position shown?'

'The Sun is in Aries, the sign of its exaltation. It is exalted. Literally, lifted up.'

'Yes, and with all the sense of exaggeration that exaltation carries. The team is playing above itself.'

'It is near the end of Aries, so it is soon to leave its exaltation. The team will fall away.'

'No. The question was asked about the present season. When a question carries an in-built time-limit, the end of the significator's present sign can be taken as that limit. So the end of Aries shows the end of the season.'

'So they will stay exalted till the end of the season.'

'Yes. But we can tell a little more than that. Which is the Sun's exaltation degree?'

'The 19th degree of Aries. 18.00-18.59 Aries.'

'So?'

'Ah! So it has passed that degree, the place where it is super-exalted. They will remain exalted, at a higher than expected position, but the best is already behind them.'

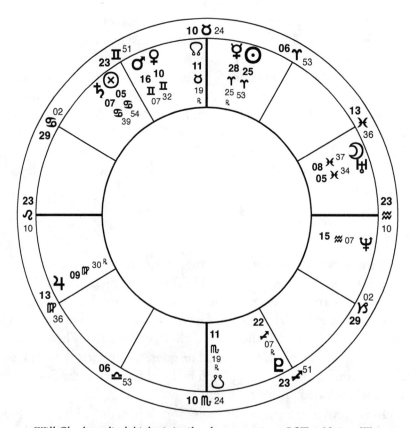

Will Charlton climb higher? April 15th 2004, 1.58 pm BST, 50N48 00W32.

'And so it proved.'

'But, Master,' he asked timidly. 'That would mean the team in a question like this would always stay at much the same level. The significator leaving its own term or face might show a slight downturn, but nothing precipitous. If the end of the sign is the end of the season, the team can't suffer a big drop in dignity.'

'It so happens that in this chart the present elevation is shown by essential dignity. In another chart this might not be the case. The planet might be leaving conjunction with the North Node and heading towards a conjunction with debilitated Saturn, for instance. That could show a big drop in fortunes.'

'Oh, I see. What about the Mercury conjunction?'

'Not relevant. It has no significant effect upon our significator. Not everything that is happening in the chart, not even everything that is happening to a main significator, needs to be taken into account. Suppose the horary question were *When*

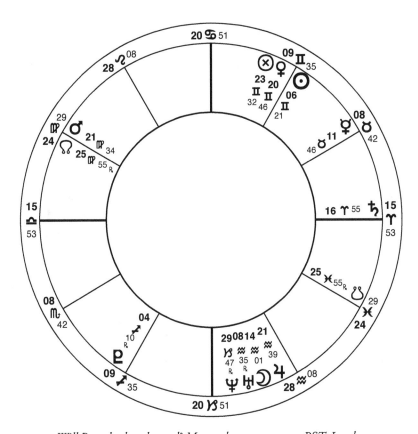

Will Barnsley be relegated? May 27th 1997, 4.10 pm BST, London.

will Granny arrive? It could well be that the Jehovah's Witnesses come to the door before she does, but this has no bearing at all on the time of her arrival.'

'That was fun, Master. Can we do another?'

Britney was growing increasingly, and vocally, impatient with her enforced still-ness, so I let her go off to graze, scratching the next chart on a rock.

'This is a question of my own. Barnsley, a small club run on a shoestring, had won promotion to the top division of English football for the first time in its history. General expectation was that it would not long survive in that affluent company. The club was at very short odds to be relegated back down at the end of the coming season. I asked: *Will Barnsley be relegated?* So, my boy: where do we begin?'

'We must start by interrogating the querent. Only by finding out his attitude towards Barnsley can we decide which house is the one to look at. Are you a Barnsley supporter, Master?'

I turned puce at the lad's impertinence. Leaping to my feet in fury, I berated him, 'I am a Master Astrologer! Long years of meditation and fasting have purified my heart till it rests like a still pool beneath the autumn Moon. How can you imagine that such idle passions as supporting Barnsley might vex my inner tranquillity?'

'Sorry, oh Master,' he whimpered.

'I did have a soft spot for them, as underdogs,' I continued, slowly recovering my composure. 'But remember the guiding rule: to give the team the 1st house, the querent must regard them as "we". Barnsley were most definitely "they". Nor,' I added, from kindness lest he invoke my wrath once more by suggesting I hated the team, 'did I see them as my enemy.'

'So you were indifferent to them. They are "any old person", and as such are shown by the 7th house.'

'Yes. Now look at the chart. First look at the 7th house itself. What do you see?'

'A seriously debilitated Saturn just inside the cusp. This is a major affliction. Bad news for Barnsley.'

'Yes. It is not a conclusive Yes to our question about relegation, but it does make it that much the more likely.'

'I suppose it's like a medical condition, Master. Testimony that the person is seriously ill is not conclusive evidence that they will die, but it does make it more likely.'

'Yes, that's right. Now, what about Lord 7?'

'That's Mars. Just entering the 12th house.'

'Which tells us what?' He looked at me blankly, so I prompted him, 'If you're stuck, always go back to the question. That gives you the context which will make sense out of the chart. What is the question about?'

'Whether Barnsley will go down.'

'And what sort of house is the 12th?'

'It's a cadent house.'

'Which means what? What does the word cadent mean?'

'Falling, Master. Oh, so they are going down!'

'Exactly. Isn't this so beautifully simple?'

'Yes, Master. Would any cadent house have shown us this?'

'Yes. Because that is what cadent means. Similarly, we might have found Lord 7 entering the sign of its fall. That too could be taken literally. That this is the 12th house serves to underline the judgement. The 12th would fittingly signify that foul pit of oblivion to which the team was so shortly to return.'

'Shouldn't we be looking at the 8th house, Master?'

'No, my boy. That would be an error in our understanding of the situation. The question is not whether the club will die, but whether it will be relegated to a lower level of competition. The financial consequences of relegation might on occasion lead to death, but in themselves the two ideas are quite distinct. Look at this one.' I scratched another chart on the rock.

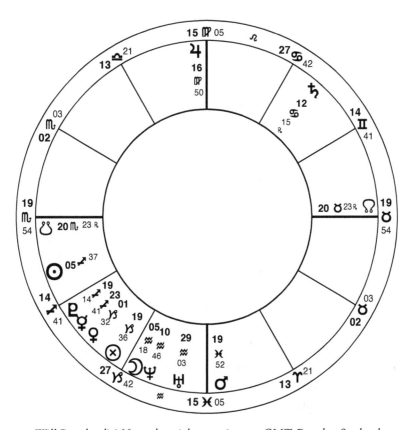

Will Dundee die? November 28th 2003, 6.50 am GMT, Dundee, Scotland.

'This querent supported Dundee United. The city's other club, Dundee, had financial problems so severe that it was threatened with closure. The question was: *Will Dundee die?* Where do we start?'

'By finding the significator. Dundee are the querent's team's local rivals. This probably makes them the enemy, and so 7th house.'

'Yes. We can't always assume that another local team will be the enemy, but that was the case here. Start by looking at the 7th house.'

'North Node close to the cusp. That's a good sign.'

'Good for Dundee, certainly,' I said, laughing. 'I'm not sure our querent would see this as good.'

'But the Node's retrograde.'

'You can ignore the Node's direction of movement. It makes no difference. Now look at Lord 7.'

'That's Venus.'

'And the significator for death?'

'Ruler of the 8th house from the 7th, the enemy's house of death. That's the radical 2nd house, ruled by Jupiter. Look at that horrible mutual reception between Jupiter and Venus, each being in the other's fall.'

'It is horrible. Venus has only recently entered Capricorn, Jupiter's fall. There must have been some recent event that has made the club fear death all the more. But fearing death is not testimony of death. Similarly with Jupiter being in its detriment. That's a nasty kind of Jupiter. But if Jupiter is Lord 8 it can still kill, no matter how dignified it might be.'

'And its placement so close to the MC?'

'That just shows that the fear of death is a real one: it may very possibly come to pass. The reverse is not true, though: if Jupiter had been in a cadent house this wouldn't show that the fear was unfounded. Which other planet must we consider?'

'I know, Master! When we're looking at somebody else's death we must consider both the turned and the radical Lord 8. Either can kill.'

'That's right. Jupiter is turned Lord 8. Radical Lord 8 is Mercury. Let's start with Mercury. Can we connect Venus to Mercury?'

He thought for a moment, then went running into the cave. He reappeared cradling his antiscion and scratching its ear. 'Venus and Mercury will conjunct by antiscion.'

'Well spotted. But an antiscion won't kill.' I twirled a blade of grass in front of its nose, while it padded at it with its paw. 'Can you connect Venus to Jupiter? That will kill.'

'Yes. Venus applies to trine Jupiter. Dundee meets death. The club folds.'

'Look again. What is Venus going to do?'

'Venus goes to oppose Saturn.'

'What does that do to the Venus/Jupiter aspect?'

'It's a prohibition, Master. It prevents Venus reaching Jupiter. There is no death.

But,' he asked, as the antiscion gnawed on his finger, 'couldn't we see that as a translation of light? Venus translates the light of Saturn to Jupiter?'

'That's an intelligent question. But no, because that translation is meaningless in this context. It would join Saturn to Jupiter, connecting whatever Saturn might signify to death. We aren't concerned with what happens to death, or with what happens to whatever Saturn might signify; we are concerned only with what happens to Dundee. If, suppose, Saturn had collected the light of Venus and Jupiter, the Saturn-thing would connect Dundee to death. That would be important. Connecting the Saturn-thing to death means nothing.'

'So Saturn saves Dundee from death. But this is a very nasty Saturn.'

'Yes, good. Saturn is in its detriment. The application is by opposition. So the saving will not be pleasant. It will not be a generous benefactor paying the club's debts. The club was put into administration, the rigour of which brought a plunge in playing fortunes. But for all those difficulties, the club survives.'

'Can we do another, Master?'

'Certainly, my boy. I applaud your enthusiasm. At the end of one season, an Arsenal supporter asked *Will my team win anything next season?* What do you think?'

'The question was asked by a fan, so Arsenal will be signified by Lord 1, which is Mercury.'

'What would show them winning something?'

'An aspect between Lord 1 and Lord 10. Or maybe between the Moon and Lord 10.'

'Avoid using the Moon as cosignificator, unless the querent is actually taking part in the competition. But an aspect between Lords 1 and 10 would be the textbook indication, yes. Is there one?'

'No. There is a strong mutual reception between them, though. That must be helpful.'

'Yes, that is most encouraging. It shows that Arsenal want success – and, more importantly, success wants Arsenal. But we still need something to show this mutual desire being turned into an event.'

'Mercury will enter its own sign. You said that the sign boundary showed the end of the time-unit....' My expression of disappointment reduced him to silence. I weighed my stick in my hand, decided I needed a sturdier for the present occasion, and went into the cave to fetch one. The impending chastisement clarified the lad's thinking, because when I was still some distance away from him he cried out, 'Oh Master, I see my error! The last season has finished, so the end of Taurus

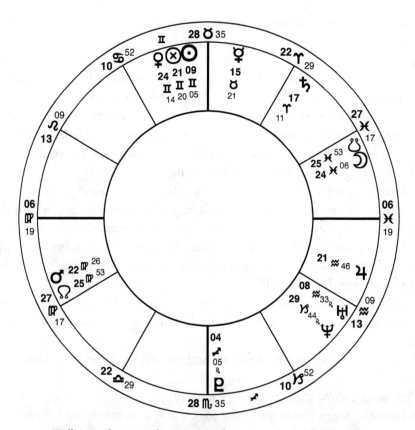

Will Arsenal win anything? May 30th 1997, 12.14 pm BST, London.

cannot be the end of that season. So if Mercury's leaving Taurus is significant, it will show the end of next season. They can't win anything after the season has finished.'

'So it can't be relevant. Exactly.' I beat him only gently, to help fix the incident in his memory. 'What is Mercury doing?'

'It's heading towards the MC. But surely that's too far off to concern us?'

'Usually, yes, we would indeed think that. Look at the number of degrees, though. It takes Mercury 13 degrees to reach the MC. Mercury was moving slightly fast at the time, so we can scale that down a bit....'[11]

'Then if each degree signifies one month, that brings Mercury to the MC in exactly a year. Right at the end of next season, when the competitions are won! So Arsenal will win something.'

[11] See the discussion of timing in *The Horary Textbook*, chapter 13.

'Yes. But what? They were entered for four competitions: one in Europe; three in England – the national league, the FA Cup, and a second knock-out tournament. Let's start with Europe. How will they fare there?'

'Debilitated Saturn on the 9th cusp: a major affliction to the house of long journeys. No success there.'

'Good. The second knock-out tournament had its final in March, only ten months away. The indicator of success shows that the success will happen in about twelve months. We can rule out that competition. This leaves us with the league and the FA Cup, both of which are decided in May.'

'I'm puzzled, Master. How can I tell?'

'We want to describe the success, so we must look at the planet that signifies success: the ruler of the 10th house. Venus itself shows the success; the sign it is in will describe that success. What kind of sign is Gemini?'

He thought for a moment, then leapt to his feet in delight. 'It's a double-bodied sign! That shows duality. They will win both!'

'And so they did.'

'Oh, Master, you predicted Arsenal would do the double? Before the season had started? Your immortal fame is indeed well-deserved!'

'Alas, no. On one TV show, *London Tonight*, I said they would win the league. On another, *Under the Moon*, that they would win the Cup. I quite failed to realise that joining these statements together showed they would win both. The art is wonderful, but there is no escaping the obtuseness of the artist.' I beat him again, to make sure he remembered that too.

'Compare this one,' I continued. It's the same question, *Will Arsenal win anything next season?* It was asked by an Arsenal fan, shortly after the end of the previous season.'

'Arsenal are shown by the 1st house again,' he began, 'because the querent is a fan. So this time they are signified by the Sun.'

'Is there any aspect to connect the Sun to the Lord of the 10th?'

'It applies to conjunct Mars, which is Lord 10.'

'Yes. But?'

'But what?' Fortunately the monk-like dedication of a Master Astrologer means I am completely bald, else I would have been tearing my hair out in handfuls. 'What happens to the Sun first?'

He looked back at the chart. 'Venus perfects its conjunction with the Sun.'

'So?'

'That's a prohibition, Master. It prohibits the Sun's conjunction with Mars.'

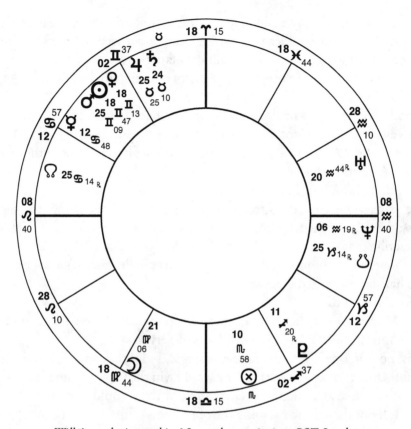

Will Arsenal win anything? June 9th 2000, 8.56 am BST, London.

'It does. But that is less important. What of the Sun/Mars conjunction itself?' He shrugged his shoulders in resignation. 'Prepare yourself, my child. The time has come for that rite of initiation that all who study with a Master Astrologer must endure.' I picked up a yak's jaw-bone that the mountain winds had been drying since before the dawn of time, and began to shape it with a flint. After some hours, while he sat in trembling expectation, the work was done. I held it over the fire until it glowed, then pressed it hard into his forehead. The words

CHECK THE EPHEMERIS

were now indelibly branded into him.

'But what does this mean, Master?'

I passed him the ephemeris. He leaved through the tattered papyrus of its well-thumbed pages. 'Oh, now I see. The Sun does not catch Mars till both planets have changed sign. Not till 10 degrees of Cancer, a third of the way through the sign. I thought it would happen much sooner.'

'That's why it is vital to check the ephemeris. What you think is going on among the planets is rarely what is really going on among the planets. You know the Sun moves faster than Mars, but you are – are you not? – surprised to see how long it takes to catch it.'

'Very surprised,' he said, obediently.

'So we find no connection between the Sun and Lord 10. Is there anything else here that might show success?'

He prowled the chart like a wolf, but could find nothing, until: 'The MC is in the degree of the Sun's exaltation.'

'Indeed it is. Well spotted. But irrelevant. Had the Sun been there, great. But it isn't. This means nothing.'

'So Arsenal won't win anything next season.'

'Nor did they. But can we see something encouraging here? After all, it's always pleasing to leave the client happy, if that can be done without distorting art. We still have the Sun/Mars conjunction, which perfects in the next sign.'

'But you said that was prohibited by Venus.'

'In terms of this season's events, which is all that is contained within the boundaries of the present sign, that conjunction is a non-starter. The limits of our question are those of the season: the sign's end. The conjunction will not happen before that. So there is really nothing for Venus to prohibit. It is prohibiting a no-thing. And prohibiting it within the bounds of this sign: this season. But...?'

'But the conjunction perfects in the next sign. Arsenal will win something next season.'

'Good. So what will they win?'

'When the conjunction is made, Mars will be...' I interrupted him. Beatings enough for one day.

'No. Where is Mars now?'

'In Gemini. A double-bodied sign. They did the double again?'

'Yes, so they did.'

'So, Master, doubles are not such a big deal. They happen all the time.'

'Only since the mid-90s. Before that they were rare. These predictions, though, were unexpected, as it seemed so unlikely that any team could so decisively breach Manchester United's dominance of English football. So unlikely that when I made that previous prediction, the interviewer on *London Tonight*, a programme inevitably biased towards the London team, Arsenal, said: "I believed everything John Frawley said, until he told me that Arsenal would win the league." A year later they replayed the interview.'

'I must remember, Master, that if the question is about events in a certain season, the end of the significator's current sign marks the end of that season.'

'Generally, yes. But you must use your common sense. If the season has just begun and the significator is at 28 degrees of its sign, the sign boundary will not show the end of the season. Discretion with art, always.'

After a pause, he began: 'We can ask if one team will win. Can we ask *which* team will win, picking the winner of the whole competition?'

'In principle this is straightforward enough. We cast the chart and look for the planet that first aspects Lord 10 or, failing that, has an immediate conjunction with the MC.'

'Simple!'

'Alas, no. The problem comes in deciding which team, or which player in an individual sport, is signified by the winning planet. This too might seem simple enough, but I have had little success. The obvious method is to use the clubs' nick-names. In British football there is a trend to dump the traditional nickname and replace it with something exciting and American-sounding. I doubt that the new names will be any help at all. Many of the traditional names, though, have a real connection with the team. The Blades, for example, originally drew their players and supporters from the steel-works, the Millers from the mills.'

'So where's the problem?'

'Consider: through recent times the top division in English football has been dominated by the Reds, the Red Devils and the Gunners.'

'Mars, Mars and Mars.'

'Then suppose the Blades make a surprise challenge for the title.'

'More Mars.'

'Quite. Consider another example, this one from Scottish football. Which planet signifies Hearts?'

'The Sun, of course.'

'Yes. Or rather, maybe. There's no "of course" about it. The club's full name is Heart of Midlothian – which was the name of a famous prison.'

'So it's Saturn.'

'But the club's nickname is the Jambos, from jam tarts, which rhymes with Hearts.'

'So it's Venus! Very confusing.'

'It's even more difficult with individuals. There are a few with clear astrological associations: Venus Williams in tennis; John Virgo in snooker. But most parents are not so cooperative. With Venus Williams, when she is on form, we can be reasonably confident that if Venus were the winning significator it would signify her, not any of the other potential Venuses in the tournament. Such occasions are rare.'

'It could be valuable to rule out such a likely winner as her.'

'True. But if we are content with that, we might as well ask *Will Venus Williams win?*'

'So is there nothing we can do with such a question?'

'Look at this one. *Who will win the Premier League?*' I didn't need to scratch up a new chart for this one, merely altering some numbers and moving the Moon.

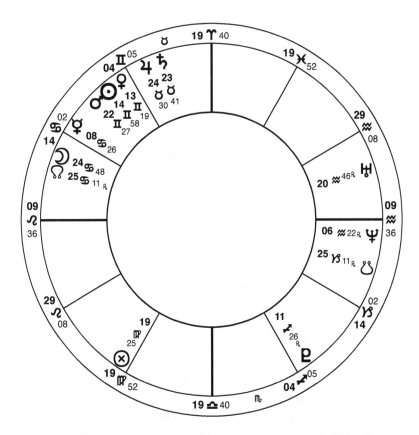

Who will win the Premier League? June 5th 2000, 9.17 am BST, London.

'Does any planet apply to aspect with Lord 10? No. We've already seen that the Sun doesn't catch Mars till well into the next sign. Does any planet apply to conjunct the MC? No. What now, then, Master?'

'Neither of our indications of victory is there. But somebody is going to win. Look at the chart as a whole. Is there anything that you notice?' He looked as blank as Britney. 'No? Look at the Moon – what about that?'

'Ah, it's void of course! Nothing will happen.'

'Well, something will assuredly happen. The tournament will take place and it will produce a winner. I've heard so much nonsense about the void of course Moon in sports charts: "Nothing will happen." "There will be no result." Huh!' Sedna flapped her wings and squawked in outrage at such foolishness. 'This can only mean that those games will never end. Even a draw is a result.'

'So what does it mean, Master?'

'It's a testimony that nothing will change. It can be overruled, but if we have no conflicting testimony there is nothing to overrule it. The team that won last season will win again. The season had just ended. Manchester United had won the league – a feat they repeated next season.'

'I'll remember that, Master. I mustn't limit my judgement to what I expect to see in the chart. I must be alert to anything the chart might suggest.'

'Good, my boy. Be alert to the context, too. Sometimes that will give us a way in to judgement. For example, the Scottish football league is almost always a two-horse race between Celtic and Rangers. Because of the religious divide, Celtic being the Catholic club, Rangers the Protestant, anyone interested enough to ask the question is likely to have a certain sympathy one way or the other, even if not enough to qualify them as a fan. So if the question *Who will win the Scottish league?* were asked, we could treat it as a straight contest, Us against Them, this contest being one that takes place over the whole season rather than over only one game.'

'I see, Master. Is it time for dinner yet?'

'Go!' And I gave him a playful buffet with my stick to send him on his way.

As we sat chewing the dry root that was our dinner, he asked, 'I am intrigued, Master, by your story about that Arsenal chart. How you made two separate, but different, predictions from the same chart. How did that happen?'

'I had done the chart for a fan. I was then asked by two TV shows to provide some predictions. Horary is always the most reliable method of predicting sports events, so where possible I would use horaries I had already done. On two separate occasions I dug out this chart. On one occasion my brain plumped one way, on the other, the other.'

He giggled. 'Sounds like you don't have much control over your brain, Master.'

'And you do? Maybe you can decide to think about a certain thing, but can you make a particular thought spring into your mind? That's why Homer is forever talking of the gods sending an idea into so-and-so's mind. If the idea isn't sent, the idea doesn't come.'

'So there's not much we can do about it.'

'Far from it. But I will tell you now the most valuable lesson in astrology that I have ever learned. It happened on the evening of May 26th, 1999. Manchester United had reached the final of the Champions' League, Europe's most prestigious club competition, to be played in Barcelona. A TV show had invited me to watch the match, making a sealed prediction of the score-line beforehand, to be opened after the game.'

'Wow, Master! A trip to Barcelona.'

'That's what I thought. But, alas, no. A trip to a sports bar in one of the less fragrant corners of London, watching the game on TV. Anyway, I cast the chart: not a horary, but a chart set for the time of kick-off. I'll tell you how to do those later. The chart showed that the favourites, Manchester United, would win. I was pretty confident about that. But I had to predict the score. That is never more than an educated guess. The chart suggested there wouldn't be many goals, but it looked as if the losers would score one. Few goals; losers score one: 2-1 seemed a likely possibility. The big problem was that the chart showed victory would come late in the game. How late? Near the end of normal time? In extra time? In a penalty shoot-out? I had to write a clear prediction: the show wasn't interested in buts or maybes.'

'Scary, Master!'

'Not really. I wasn't much concerned. I had nothing to prove. Whether the prediction was right or wrong would tell absolutely nothing about either the validity of the technique or my abilities as an astrologer. It would prove nothing except, for whatever reason, that prediction had been right or wrong. And this wasn't confrontational TV. The programme was to be shown at a later date. If I'd been wrong, they may well have cut it. After all, "Astrologer Gets it Wrong!" isn't headline news.'

'True.'

'But so many people were involved. The presenter, director, camera-crew, lighting- and sound-crews: they had all schlepped to this Godforsaken part of London for the event. I did feel I would have been letting the side down if I'd got it wrong.'

'So what did you do, Master?'

'I did all that an astrologer can ever do. I put it all in the hands of Our Lady, asking her for the grace to do as should be done. I wrote the prediction and gave it to the landlord of the pub. With a great deal of fanfare, he locked it in his safe.'

'What happened?'

'With 90 minutes gone, Manchester United were losing 1-0. United had played badly; their opponents, Bayern Munich, had controlled the whole game. All that remained were three minutes added on for injuries. The pub, of course, was full of United fans, so the atmosphere was funereal. The dispassionate astrologer was filmed assuring them there was plenty of time yet. United scored, and everyone readied themselves for extra time. United scored again. The final whistle blew. The most remarkable ending to a match that most of us had ever seen. The safe was opened and the prediction revealed: Manchester United to win 2-1 in normal time.'

'Oh, Master! Brilliant!'

'Well, not really. A sound knowledge of astrology and the grace to make the right choices. That was my big lesson: no matter how profound our knowledge, how steady our concentration, we can never force two thoughts to join together. All is done by grace. What I'm teaching you can provide some of the knowledge. If you work at it, practice, practice, practice, that amount will grow. I must refer you elsewhere for the grace.'

Next morning, early, I plucked some more leaves from the mountain palm at the mouth of the cave, and drew some charts. 'Try these on your own,' I told him. 'You'll find the judgements in Appendix 4.'

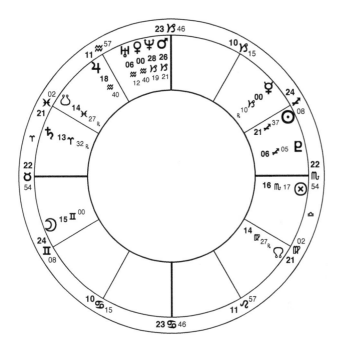

Test chart 1. Will my team win this match? December 13th 1997, 2.14 pm GMT, London.

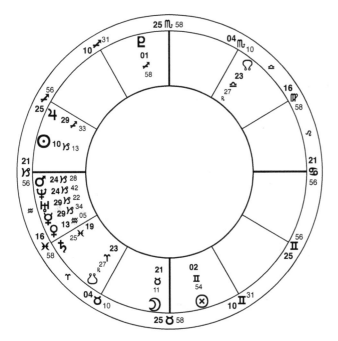

Test chart 2. Will (named team) win this tournament? The querent neither supported nor disliked the team, asking only out of curiosity. January 1st 1996, 8.54 am GMT, London.

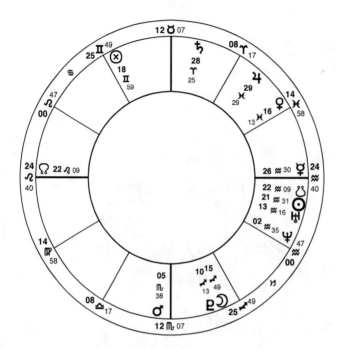

Test chart 3. Will my team win this match? February 10th 1999, 5.18 pm GMT, London.

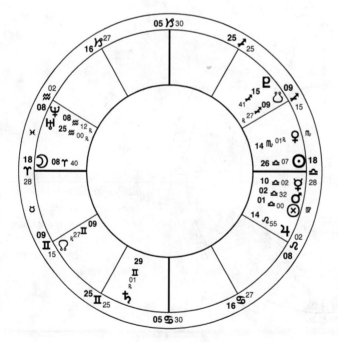

Test chart 4. Will my team be relegated? The team finishing the season bottom of the division would be relegated to the division below. October 19th 2002, 5.44 pm BST, Dundee, Scotland.

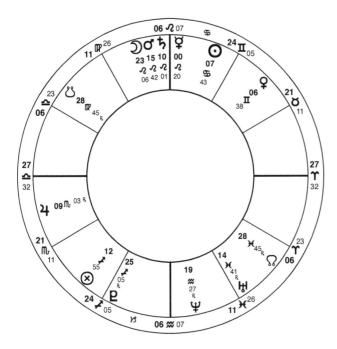

Test chart 5. Will the champ win this match? June 29th 2006, 3.26 pm BST, 50No7 5W32.

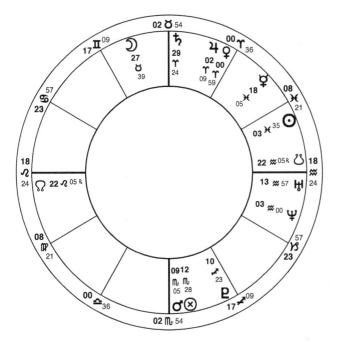

Test chart 6. Will my team win promotion? At the end of the current season, four teams at the top of the league would be promoted to the league above. February 22nd 1999, 3.55 pm GMT, London.

INTERLUDE:

'THE SPORTSMAN OF THE CENTURY'[12]

The 7th house of a birthchart, in particular the cusp of that house, is the point that most clearly marks the native's engagement with the world. A planet within a degree or two of that cusp will have a dominant influence on the way that person relates with others, both 'significant others' and the insignificant others that make up the world in general. If there is a planet placed thus, this will usually be what an acquaintance would pick up on if asked to describe the native.

It might, then, be a surprise to find Venus so placed in the nativity of a man famous for hitting people, and hitting them hard. Yet if we remember the warm affection with which Muhammad Ali is regarded – quite a contrast from such fearsome characters as Mike Tyson – this placement becomes less of a puzzle. Hitting people may have been what he did, for what he was admired, for what he became famous, but the image that remains is not that of a man of violence.

Placed as it is, Venus opposes the Ascendant, the native's own part of the chart. With Venus ruling the 10th house, this shows the conflicts Ali would face with authority, both within and without his chosen sport. Its mutual reception with Lord 7, his enemies, is eloquent: it was not an opponent, but the authorities, who first took his title from him.

A planet in tight aspect with the Ascendant, as Venus is, will have an important influence on the native's appearance. This planet being Venus, and it being in Aquarius, which is a voiced sign, it is no surprise to hear him so often proclaiming 'I'm so pretty!'

The Ascendant itself falls on the fixed star Algenubi, which will therefore colour the native's character. Algenubi is in the constellation of Leo, so we might expect some powerful acts of violence, as befits the king of beasts. Within that constellation, it is in the lion's mouth, so we should expect not only ferocity, irresistible power, heartless rending, but also a good deal of ferocious noise. That is what a lion's mouth does. Which two planets, combined, would portray a heavyweight

---

[12] As named by *Sports Illustrated* and the BBC.

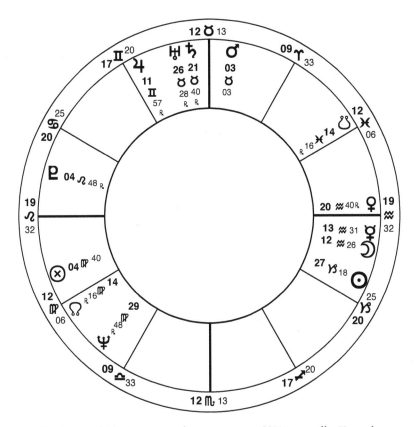

Muhammad Ali, January 17th 1942, 6.35 pm CST, Louisville, Kentucky.

boxer? Surely Mars and Saturn. The nature of Algenubi is, as Ptolemy tells us, a combination of Mars and Saturn.[13] According to Vivian Robson, the authority on fixed stars, Algenubi 'gives a bold, bombastic, cruel, heartless, brutish and destructive nature, but artistic appreciation and power of expression'.[14] Venus may take the edge off some of these indications – though his prolonged destruction of Ernie Terrell in 1967 was still 'a barbarous display of cruelty'[15] – but as a pen-picture of the Louisville Lip, Robson's delineation of Algenubi is not far from the mark.

All the angles and five of the seven planets being in fixed signs provides the resilience necessary to fight on for ten rounds after Ken Norton had broken his

[13] Claudius Ptolemy, *Tetrabiblos*, p. 49; trans Robbins, Harvard UP, 1940.
[14] Vivian Robson, *The Fixed Stars and Constellations in Astrology*, p. 123; London, 1923, reprinted Nottingham, n.d.
[15] In the opinion of journalist Tex Maule, http://en.wikipedia.org/wiki/Muhammad_Ali.

jaw, and on which Ali's rope-a-dope strategy relied. The significator of his opponents is Saturn, ruler of the 7th house. Currently retrograde, Saturn is about to change direction and begin moving forwards. To do that, it has to slow to a stop, 'entering station'. As a planet loses speed it loses strength, as if it were tiring. So if Ali can draw his opponents into using their strength to no purpose, as he lies back on the ropes absorbing all they can throw at him, they will tire. And so it proved.

Ali, meanwhile, has speed in abundance. With Saturn, most ponderous of planets, in Taurus, most ponderous of signs, as significator of his opponents, it would not need much for him to appear faster. But there is much. The ruler of the 1st house, main significator of Ali himself, is the Sun. The Sun's speed never significantly varies, so we cannot ever regard it as moving fast or slow. The significator of Ali's feet, however, tells a different story. The feet are shown by the 12th house, which here is ruled by the Moon. When Ali was born, the Moon was moving exceptionally fast, at well over 14 degrees a day. Fast feet. Closely conjunct nimble Mercury, we see the famous Ali shuffle:

> *Float like a butterfly, sting like a bee,*
> *Your hands can't hit what your eyes can't see.*

2

The chart for the event

'Oh, brave my Master! Now I have fathomed horary, no knowledge shall lie beyond my questing mind. What can I not do now!'

'Quite a lot, young man,' I replied, sorting through my sticks for one sturdy enough to disabuse him of such extravagance. 'Beyond even your own fallibility, and that is great, there are limitations in the art itself.'

'Never!' he cried. 'That cannot be. How can this celestial art have limitation? Is there something you withhold from me, some dark arcana you divulge only...'

'...to the ones with Amex?' I interrupted. 'No. The only different tuition they receive is the use of a bigger stick. Though the art may be celestial, the artist is yet mundane, penned in among the possibilities of mortal life. This world is not divine. It is not perfect. Nor is there a perfect refuge from it in astrology. While we may study the stars we remain on Earth.'

'And you, Master, never will I believe that you are fallible.' I took a swing at him and missed, to prove my point. 'So what are these limitations in horary?' he asked, rubbing his shoulder from my second swing.

'All astrology should be used sparingly, my boy. That much, I hope you have wit enough to have realised by now. Salt adds to the flavour of a dish, but is a vile dish in itself. This is especially true of horary, while horary, being so easy to use, can easily tempt the unwary to overuse it. There are the lovelorn, who will ask *Is it this one? Is it this one?* about any man they meet. There are the ragged actors, asking *Is it this one? Is it this one?* about every audition they attend. This is not astrology, but impotence hoping for magic. It is not to be encouraged, because that magic cannot be provided. Indeed, the cosmos appears to lose interest after two or three such enquiries. On your journey to my cave you no doubt passed diviners using the *I Ching*.' He nodded. 'So you will perhaps recall the hexagram which says "You didn't take any notice last time, so why are you bothering me now?" Horary charts react in a similar way, making it obvious they have no intention of responding to the question.'

'But surely it is possible to ask the same question more than once?'

'It is no more possible to ask the same question, strictly speaking, than it is to step twice into the same stream. But I understand your meaning. Yes, people do ask repeated questions on some pressing subject. But we are expected to get the message after a while. A horary should teach us something beyond the information directly requested: either that this information was not so important after all, or that we can sense all we need know by cutting out the astrological middleman and engaging directly with the situation ourselves. We may ask that weather-wise old sea-dog if a storm is brewing, but once he's pointed out identical cloud formations to us on three or four occasions, politeness dictates that we leave him to his pipe and gauge the portents ourselves. The stars deserve the same consideration.'

'So what happens if someone does repeatedly ask the same question?'

'After a while – after quite a short while – the stars lose interest. They pick up their ball and go home.'

'So it's like the fairy-tales, where the good fairy gives you three wishes, and that's all you're getting?'

'Not quite. But horary does need to be used with discretion. Consider: we have one fan who asks *Will my team win?* when they play the grudge match against their local rivals. Then repeats the question when they are pitted against the mighty Superstars United in a knock-out competition. Then again before the crucial end-of-season match which will determine which league they play in next season. Or we have another fan who asks *Will my team win?* before every game. There's a big difference: one is a reasonable use of horary, the other is not. Even more of a difference if that second fan starts asking the question twice before games, because he didn't like the answer he got the first time.'

'Right, Master. We can't ask the same question on every trivial occasion. And you've already told me that we can't use horary when the querent has no preference for one or other team.'

'Yes. The well-equipped sports astrologer will have the foresight to fill a cupboard with supporters of a large number of different teams, each of them ready to pop out at a moment's notice to ask a horary question about that team's next match. Those not provident enough to do this will soon bump into the limitations of horary. Indeed, these limitations are more apparent in the field of sports than in any other area of enquiry.'

'I thought horary was such an excellent method.'

'It is. It is by far the most reliable method, but it is only for special occasions. If we wish to predict sports on a day-to-day basis, we need another technique.'

'I know! I know!' he cried, bouncing up and down like a yo-yo. 'We can use birthcharts.'

'Ah yes – the birthchart approach. How do you propose we do this?'

'We look at transits to the charts of the participants. That will show us who has a successful day and who loses.'

I looked at my stick and weighed it carefully in my hand. Disappointed, I decided it was not sturdy enough to deliver the thrashing an answer like that deserved, for all that there are astrologers who claim, apparently in all seriousness, to use this method. 'Let us consider a football match. There are eleven players in each team, plus five substitutes, who may or may not take part in the game. The teams will often not be announced until shortly before kick-off. This gives you thirty-two charts to study, up to ten of which might be irrelevant – but you don't know how many and which these are. Then let's include the charts of the managers. That's a lot of charts. You have timed charts for all of them? I doubt it. Then we would have to study these charts.'

'That's easy. All we need know is where the planets are on the day.'

' Yes, transits.' I snapped my fingers and Sedna came hopping towards me carrying an ancient leather-bound volume in his beak. 'Behold, my boy: *Ye Dictionary of Astrologie.*' I opened it and read, 'Transit: Babylonian word meaning "I'm too lazy to do proper astrology".' He looked at me as if I had trodden on his favourite toy.

'William Lilly's *Christian Astrology* runs to some 850 pages. He devotes three paragraphs to transits, and that is about two and a half paragraphs more than they deserve.[16] Yet to hear some astrologers speak, you would think the whole art of prediction was encompassed there. You have studied transits?'

'Indeed, Master.'

'And you have never noticed how the Saturn transit you were dreading produces....nothing? And the Jupiter transit you awaited so eagerly produces.... nothing? With sports, the transit-fans are especially fond of Mars transits. According to Lilly, a Mars transit 'moves the native to choler or passion'.[17] If someone's playing professional sports, I would hope he did have his pulses racing! Does this transit tell us anything beyond that?'

'So what use are transits?'

[16] p. 741.
[17] p. 741.

'Precious little. And that is so whatever the subject of our astrological investigation. Transit-fans treat astrology as a form of bibliomancy: open the ephemeris and behold, you have a prediction! There is more to it than that. Transits mean nothing without a context. We must first study – and thoroughly – the birthchart. Without knowing exactly what, for example, Jupiter means and how it is configured in that chart, we can have no idea of what Jupiter might signify in transit. It is far more than the celestial version of Santa Claus. Which houses does it rule in the nativity? How dignified is it? How does it relate to the other planets by reception? If we can answer these questions, we might see that a Jupiter transit is the last thing that would bring this native success. Only once we have gained an understanding of the natal chart can we begin the process of predicting from it.'

'That sounds like a lot of work.'

'It is a lot of work. How interested are you in the outcome of this game? And we have hardly even begun. Next we must consider the progressions and the return charts. Progressions are the cake; the return charts are the icing. Transits? They are merely the cherry on the top. Take the cherry away and the cake would taste much the same.'

'You mean I have to do all that with thirty-four charts? Master, I did not take up astrology from a love of hard labour.'

'The hard labour is only the beginning. It is not enough to toil vigorously; you must also develop subtlety in judgement. So you see that the team's star has the game of his life; he can still lose. This is true even of one-on-one contests. Or perhaps you have a journeyman player. Walking onto the same turf as his heroes in the opposing team is the greatest moment of his sporting life. Beside that, his team's defeat means nothing. Or you see the striker has a disastrous day. He is injured and never plays again – but he scored the winning goal. Or the team loses, but after the match the player signs a lucrative new contract, so it's a successful day for him, despite the defeat.'

'It's complicated.'

'And we must never forget that sportsmen are human too. For the fan screaming on the terraces this match might be something special. For the player it is one more day at the office. More significant than the result, to him, might be the row he had with the manager before the game. The Jupiter transit you think wins him the match means his wife gives birth. That Saturn square is his car breaking down.'

'Oh, Master, let's not do predictions from the natal charts.'

'Very wise, my boy.' He assumed that expression of profound thoughtfulness, gazing vacantly into the middle distance, that I had come to realise meant I had said enough. A certain twitching in his fingers, though, I had also come to recognise. 'You have a question?'

'Master, I see now that using transits is wrong. Please beat me for my foolishness.'

'You are a student,' I said, trying my best at a benevolent smile, 'It's your job to get things wrong.' I smacked him over the shoulder with my stick, but my heart was not in it.

He now came to his question. 'But Master, if it is too much work to study the birthcharts of all the players, can we not use the birthchart for the team? Or suppose we have a one-on-one contest. Can't we use the natal charts then?'

'You do like hard work, don't you?' I opened a bottle of the finest high-grown Himalayan Malbec to fortify myself against the very thought of expending this amount of effort on a sports prediction. Sufficiently fortified, I began, 'We have two situations here. The one-on-one individual contest and the clash of teams. Let us begin by considering the one-on-one contest.' I rapped him across the knuckles to make sure he was paying attention. 'Yes, my boy, in a one-on-one contest the nativities can tell us everything. If you do all the work I've just listed. And if you bear in mind certain realities, which are so often forgotten.'

'I am a student of astrology, oh Master. Reality is a place I rarely visit. What do you mean?'

'Let us take an example from the world of politics. Not so long ago the good citizens of America chose who would ignore their wishes for the next four years. The incumbent president, George Bush, ran against John Kerry. Astrologers crawled from every crack and crevice to predict the outcome.'

'I remember that well, Master. Few of them were right.'

'Yes. We may discount the many who saw nothing more in the stars than their own wishful thinking. But even among those who judged the contest dispassionately, there was a common error: too much astrology; too little reality. The failure, as the great William Lilly would have put it...' The boy leapt to his feet and saluted. '...to combine discretion with art.'

'How so, Master?'

'Astrologers would study Kerry's chart, its progressions, returns and yes, alas, its transits, and find some strong positive testimonies. They would therefore conclude that he must win.'

'So what's wrong with that?'

'What's wrong is that the astrological investigation does not match the reality of the situation. A year or so earlier few people had heard of Kerry. On election night, he was on every TV in the world. He came within one state of becoming president. Of course his chart showed success: win or lose, this will probably prove to have been the most successful night of his life.'

'I see. In another field of contest he might have got a silver medal and been happy.'

'Exactly. Whatever the political theory might be, in practical terms there was an incumbent president. No matter how well Kerry does, he cannot win unless there is a change in the status quo. If Bush does not lose, Kerry cannot win. There will not be a vacancy in the White House for Kerry to fill.'

'So the astrological investigation would have to start with Bush's chart. If that doesn't show him losing, we don't need even to look at Kerry's.'

'Yes, we need to see testimony of Bush losing. Or maybe of him moving house, because the house goes with the job. There was no such testimony.'

'So even though this appears to be a straight contest, we can't judge it as such.'

'Correct. We must think clearly about the nature of the contest. Tell me, boy, what is the difference between a contest like that, or a boxing title-fight, and, say, the final of the Australian Open?'

His expression showed thoughts trudging round inside his head, while Sedna hopped from foot to foot with caws of 'I know! I know!' I let the bird whisper the answer – correct, of course – into my ear, before turning back to the lad. 'In a title fight,' I explained, 'the situation is the same as with Bush and Kerry. No matter how well the challenger does, if the champion doesn't lose there is no vacancy. In the Aussie Open it is different. Even if one of the finalists won last year's Open, he is not currently the champion.'

'So we could compare the nativities?'

'We could. But we've already spoken about the limitations of that – to say nothing of the amount of work it involves. If this is the one final that these players have ever reached, we might expect some technicolour testimonies in the chart. But if this is the one final they have ever reached, we would expect powerful testimonies even in the loser's chart. Being runner-up is still pretty good. While if the chart is of a Martina Navratilova, winning Open after Open, we would not expect every victory to be marked by astrological fireworks. It's just another day at the office.'

'But we should be able to look at the chart to see who will perform better on the day.'

'So what? Maybe you'd like to have a flying contest with Sedna. Sedna's chart could show any number of afflictions. He could do the worst piece of flying he has ever done. You could flap your arms more energetically than ever before. He'll still beat you.'

'OK, Master, so we'll forget individuals' birthcharts. Can we look at the birthchart for a team?'

'This sounds a good idea, my boy, but I have not found it successful. This is probably mainly because of the difficulty of finding the significant chart. After all, most sports clubs were born as a bunch of lads playing ball on a patch of waste ground. The official charts usually relate to the club as a business rather than to the club as a bunch of lads playing a game, which is what concerns us.'

'So why can't we take the chart for a moment of sporting, rather than business, significance?'

'More often than not, any significant initiating moment is lost in the mists of memory. Even when we have the date of a club's first match, we rarely know the time of kick-off.'

'So what can we use, then, Master? Can we cast a chart for the match itself and predict from that?'

'Yes. The problem here being the problem with any event chart: who gets which house?'

'I've heard that the instigator of the event gets the 1st house.'

'And you thought that was a good idea? Consider: if a dog bites you and you decide to cast a chart for that event, who gets the 1st house?'

'The dog, I suppose, Master. That's who instigated the action.'

'But suppose the dog bit you because you trod on its tail. Who instigated the action then?'

'It's not so simple, is it, Master?'

'Indeed not. It has been said that we can do this in event charts for contests.[18] But we cannot. The action is mutually instigated. Lee Lehman gives the example of baseball, where the home team makes the first pitch. But the visiting team could equally well be said to make the instigating action, merely by turning up.'

'So what about the team that wins the toss? Or which kicks off?'

I had been gentle with the lad for too long; my laxity was beginning to affect his wits. After a suggestion like that I had to boil his head. Dousing him in the cooking-pot for a couple of minutes did have a salutary effect on his thinking, but the odd flavour it imparted to the stew deterred me from using that method of correction again.

[18] by e.g. J. Lee Lehman in *Predicting the Outcome of Games or Confrontations: Where to Start*, in *The Horary Practitioner*, vol 9, issue 24, 1998.

'You are familiar with the word *pre*diction?' I asked him, when he had dried off.
'Yes, Master.'

'If we are to *pre*dict something, it is useful if we do it before the event.'
'Yes, Master.'

'It is tempting to use natural rulers: Mars for the Red Sox; Moon for the White Sox. But this doesn't work – to say nothing of the problem I've mentioned before, of what happens when the Reds play the Reds, or the Gunners play the Red Devils.'

'I've heard that giving the home team the Ascendant works.'

'And I've heard that the Moon is made of cream cheese. This doesn't work, no matter how much people may insist on it.'

'So what, then?'

'Lehman suggests that many contests can be judged using a method based on Bonatti's instructions for forecasting the outcome of a siege.[19] I disagree. The siege metaphor is not a relevant one. For instance, she claims that the home team can often be regarded as the besieged party, because in most sports the home team wins more often than the visiting team. But suppose my country is invading your country. If my army sits down around your capital, that is a siege. If my army fights a pitched battle with your army, the fact that your army is playing at home doesn't make that a siege: it is a pitched battle. She argues that the home team has an advantage, therefore it is a siege. But there is no "therefore" here. There are many factors that make an army more likely to win a battle. The army holding the higher ground has an advantage over the army that must attack uphill. The army that arrived on the field first, thus giving itself the choice of ground, has an advantage. But neither these nor any other factors convert a pitched battle into a siege.'

'I see.'

'Lehman also applies the siege method to those situations like title fights, where the champion remains champion merely by avoiding defeat, just as a besieged city does not have to defeat its attackers – the populace can sit tight and wait for the enemy to go away. But a title fight is still not a siege. Siege means "sitting down": the army sits down at the gates of a city. It would be unusual to see a boxer attempting to win the title by sitting down at the feet of the champion and waiting for him to surrender, or, indeed, for the champion to sit and do nothing in hope that the challenger will eventually go away. It is the wrong metaphor. A champion versus challenger match is not a 4th-house matter – *will the city withstand the siege?* – but a 10th-house matter: *will the king will be deposed?*'

'OK, so what do we do, Master?'

[19] ibid.

The Method

'Set the chart for the time and place of kick-off. Use Placidus houses, as with any event chart. Give the favourite the 1st house and the underdog the 7th.'

'Why?'

'Because it works.'

'How do I know which is favourite?'

'If you are interested enough to be looking at the chart, your knowledge of the sport will often tell you this. If not, check with the bookies.'

He looked troubled. 'But Master, are bookmakers really such paragons that we can admit them as arbiters among the celestial spheres?'

'It would be nice if angelic hands were to unfurl a banner across the sky telling us which team was truly favourite, but those hands seem to be fully occupied on other business, so we must make do. The bookies' odds are the best measure we have. They are usually reliable enough, though there are certain cautions. Remember that the purpose of these odds is to tempt Joe Punter to place a bet, so they do not exactly reflect the bookie's opinion on which team is most likely to win. Suppose, for example, a team from your country were to play a bunch of dastardly foreigners.'

'Oh, my brave boys! I'd back them to beat that dreadful crew any day.'

'And so would many another, with no careful consideration of the true merits of the teams. So the odds on the team from your country might be a little slimmer than is truly warranted. You might bear this in mind if the odds on each team were more or less equal.'

'What if the odds are equal, Master, so there is no favourite?'

'Too bad. We can't use this method.' He looked most put out, poor lad, with wings of expectation beating in vain. 'We can't do everything. Rejoice in what we can do, don't mourn for what we cannot.'

'So, Master: 1st house for the favourites; 7th for the underdog.'

'Give the favourites the 10th as well, and the underdog the 4th. The 4th being the 10th house from the 7th, so each team also has its respective house of success. The other houses are neutral.'

'So we weigh up the strength of the significators?'

'I'm glad you asked that, my boy, because it allows me to emphasise a most important point,' which I did, smacking him firmly and rhythmically around the back of his head to drive home the meaning:

IT'S NOT THE SAME AS HORARY
DON'T MIX THE METHODS

I repeated this, just in case. Twice.

'We are down at the bottom of the astrological food-chain here,' I continued. 'There is a hierarchy in astrological method. The higher the level, the more ponderous are the techniques that are appropriate for it. With horary, for example, which is one of the lower levels, the Moon is important; fixed stars are usually not. By the time we climb to mundane astrology, the Moon plays only a tiny role, its swift motion being altogether too fleeting to matter much there, while such slow-moving beasts as fixed stars and the cycle of Grand Conjunctions come to the fore.'

At the mention of slow-moving beasts, Britney twitched in her sleep, as if I might want something from her. I patted her in reassurance, and she soon settled again. 'Here, we are at a level below even horary. It's as if we were studying some primitive life-forms that have but few faculties, revealing their presence only by the occasional flash of dim light in a pitch-dark cave. So it is with these charts. Small measures of movement and certain narrowly prescribed house-placements are all that concern us.'

'Such as?'

EVENT-CHART CHECKLIST

For the favourite: 1st house and 10th house
For the underdog: 7th house and 4th house

Check:

house placement of:	Lords 1, 7, 4 and 10
	Moon
	Part of Fortune (by antiscion only!)
aspects to or from:	Moon
	Part of Fortune (bodily and by antiscion)
	dispositor of the Part of Fortune
miscellaneous points:	the Nodes
	combustion
	the outer planets

'First, check for **house placement**. We are looking at Lords 1, 4, 7 and 10. Is any of these close to the cusp of any of these four houses?'

'How close?'

'Very close. Sitting on the cusp, at most a couple of degrees before it. Tucked just inside the house, at most a couple of degrees inside it.'

'That's very limiting. Surely this means that in most charts there will be no testimony like this?'

'That's right. There is no purpose in accumulating testimonies for the sake of accumulating testimonies. Let us limit ourselves to what is significant. Now, remember:

A PLANET ON A CUSP CONTROLS THAT HOUSE
A PLANET INSIDE A CUSP IS CONTROLLED BY THAT HOUSE

So:

* Lord 1 sitting on the 7th cusp is strong testimony that the favourite will win.
* Lord 1 just inside the 7th house is strong testimony the favourite will lose.
* Lord 7 on the 1st cusp favours the underdog.
* Lord 7 just inside the 1st house shows the underdog in the favourite's power.

Similarly with the other houses under consideration. For instance:

* Lord 10 on 7th cusp favours the favourite.
* Lord 10 inside 7th house favours the underdog.
* Lord 7 on 10th cusp favours the underdog.
* Lord 7 inside 10th house favours the favourite.

And so on.'

'What about planets on or in their own houses?'

'These are important, too. But these testimonies are less strong than those involving the enemy's house. For example, Lord 1 either on the 1st cusp or inside the 1st house is strengthened, but although strengthened this lacks the sense of being strengthened vis-à-vis the enemy that comes from its dominating the 7th house. One is like a champion waving his sword at one end of the jousting field; the other is like a champion waving his sword with one foot on his enemy's neck.'

'So Lord 10 on or in the 10th is testimony for the favourite.'

'Yes.'

'And Lord 4 on or in the 4th favours the underdog.'

'Yes.'

'Suppose the planet is retrograde, Master?'

'If it is retrograde and inside one of its enemy's houses, the retrogradation makes no difference: it is still in the power of its enemy. If it is retrograde and sitting on the cusp of one of its enemy's houses, this is still a positive testimony, but less strong than if it were in the same position and direct.'

'And those little creatures, Master – what about them?'

'Good! Yes, my boy, antiscia are important here. Perhaps not quite so compelling in testimony as bodily placements, but certainly worth noting. So:

* Antiscion of Lord 1 on 7th cusp favours the favourite.
* Antiscion of Lord 1 inside 7th house favours the underdog.

And similarly with all the other permutations.'

'What about other house placements?'

'Irrelevant.'

'Lord 1 being in a cadent house?'

'Irrelevant!'

'A significator in the 12th?'

A hearty thump with my stick finally got my point across. 'Irrelevant. Irrelevant. Irrelevant! Even if there are no other testimonies in the chart – still irrelevant! Do you doubt that I meant what I said about these charts? That we work with only the most limited palette here?

FORGET ESSENTIAL DIGNITY
FORGET ACCIDENTAL DIGNITY
FORGET RECEPTIONS

They simply don't work in these charts. Beyond the tight parameters I gave you, of some 2 or 3 degrees before or after the cusp, position by house means nothing. Lord 1 is not mildly afflicted by being 6 degrees inside the 7th house; it is not afflicted at all. Lord 1 might be 6 degrees inside the 1st house while Lord 7 is tucked away inside the 12th: this means nothing.'

'Why is this, Master?'

'Because we need such a sensitive instrument for this investigation. Consider: horary questions about sport can be asked at any hour of day or – if the astrologer does not take precautions – night. The matches themselves, however, begin only at a limited range of times. Especially if we are concerned only with one particular sport. If this evening's game kicks off at 7.30, it is likely that tomorrow's game will kick off at 7.30, and the game next Monday, and the one on Friday week. If we allowed these slow-changing testimonies into judgement, we would give all these matches the same result: favourite win or favourite lose. That does not happen.'

'So we must go for the ephemeral.'

'Exactly. Suppose we look at an evening kick-off with Aquarius rising. Saturn rules the favourites, the Sun the underdogs. Suppose Saturn is in Leo. If we judged by reception, it would take an unusual combination of testimonies to outweigh that. The favourites would lose. In match after match after match. And because Saturn spends two and a half years in each sign, there would be exactly the same run of surprise results at exactly the same time next year.'

'OK, Master. What do we do next?'

'Next we look at **the house placement of the Moon**. The Moon does not stand for either team. My best description of it is that

THE MOON SHOWS THE FLOW OF EVENTS

* Moon applying to or close inside the 1st or 10th cusp: victory goes to the favourite.
* Moon applying to or close inside the 7th or 4th cusp: victory goes to the underdog.
* Consider its antiscion too.'

'It seems like the Moon being in one team's house is like a big surge of energy towards that team, almost as if the cosmos is cheering for it.'

'That's about it, my boy. Nicely put!'

'And if it's somewhere else in the chart? In the 2nd house, say, or the 5th?'

'Irrelevant. We've finished with the Moon. Next look at **the house placement of Fortuna**.'

'I'm getting the hang of this, Master. Let me have a go. The Part of Fortune just inside the 1st house shows the favourite winning; just inside the 7th shows the favourite losing.'

'Alas, no. Judging Fortuna is not quite so straightforward. Remember that one way of looking at the Part of Fortune is as a way of marking the phase of the Moon in the chart. At New Moon Fortuna is exactly on the Ascendant. Through the lunar month it then works its way round the chart in an anticlockwise direction, until at Full Moon it is exactly on the Descendant. In the second half of the month it completes its anticlockwise journey back to the Ascendant.'

'So if what I said was true, the favourites would win any game starting at around New Moon, and they would lose any game starting around Full Moon.'

'Yes. That doesn't happen. If it did, we might have expected folk wisdom to have noticed.'

He looked thoughtful, then a sly smile came into his eyes. 'I know, Master – it's those little animals again, isn't it? You love them little animals.'

'They are quite cute, I will admit. But they can give you a nasty nip. My affection for them is only because they work so well in charts. Yes, you're right: we must look to the antiscion.

ANTISCION OF FORTUNA, NOT BODILY PLACEMENT

Although the Part of Fortune continues its stately progress round the chart as the month unfolds, its antiscion leaps about all over the place. It can appear anywhere, at any time of the month. As for what it means, you've got the general idea by now:

* Antiscion of Fortuna close to 1st cusp: favourite wins.
* Antiscion of Fortuna close to 7th cusp: favourite loses.
And so on.'

'It's only an antiscion, so I suppose it's not such a strong testimony.'

I clapped him round the ear. 'You're lucky those little fellows are back in the cave, so none of them can hear you. There's no "only" about it! If the antiscion of Fortuna is in a significant position, it is one of the most powerful single testimonies in judging these charts. Perhaps the most powerful of all.'

'Do I reverse the calculation of Fortuna in night charts?'

'Never! There are profounder reasons for not doing so, but also two that relate directly to our conversation here. One is that the position of Fortuna is a charting of the Moon's phase throughout the month. The Moon's phase does not change as soon as it gets dark. The other is from experience. Fortuna has such a significant role in these charts that many times we judge by it alone. I have consistently drawn accurate judgement using the daytime calculation, whether by day or by night.'

'What about other Arabian Parts – the Part of Victory, perhaps?'

'I've never used them. I've seen others doing so, but have been unconvinced. If you wish to experiment with them when you leave here, by all means do so, but I've never felt their lack. After all, how much work do you want to do?'

That gave him thought, so I paused before continuing: 'We shall now move on to **aspects**.'

'Aha! Lord 1 squares Lord 7: favourite wins!'

'No, my boy, no. Aspects between our main significators will be rare, because they will concern us only if they are close. But even if there is such an aspect, remember that we are paying no heed to accidental dignity, essential dignity or reception. So we have no way of deciding which of the two aspecting planets will come off the better.'

'So I should ignore aspects between Lords 1 and 7?'

'Yes – with one exception. If we are judging a horary chart for a court-case, the antagonists' significators coming into aspect tells us that they will settle out of court. In most sports charts such a conclusion is impossible: if the Yankees are playing the Red Sox we can assume that the players will not settle their differences midway through the game and adjourn to the nearest bar. If our chart is for a chess match, however, we can take an aspect between Lords 1 and 7 as testimony of a draw. All other testimonies agreeing, that is: if one player is in a greatly superior position this testimony will probably be overruled.'

'So in a boxing match, when the corner throws in the towel?'

'That is not a draw, dear boy; that is surrender.'

'Right, Master. Now, if we're not interested in those aspects... I know! You said we are concentrating on the most ephemeral things. That means the Moon's aspects must be important.'

'Yes! Although house placement can be decisive, meaningful house placements do not occur in most charts. **The Moon's aspects** probably decide a greater proportion of these charts than any other testimony. We are, of course, concerned only with *applying* aspects: aspects that have not already happened. And we are concerned with them over only a limited range, which will vary with the sport, including differences between the different codes of football:

football (80 minutes or more):	maximum 5 degrees add 1 degree if extra time is possible
football (less than 80 minutes):	maximum 4 degrees add 1 degree if extra time is possible
cricket (1-day):	maximum 13 degrees
cricket (county or test):	until end of Moon's present sign

When judging other sports I've achieved good results by sticking to the 5-degree limit. That includes tennis, where top-flight matches will usually last rather longer than a football match. If you are judging a lot of tennis or baseball matches, you may find experience leads you to extend that limit a little.'

'You're saying that if the Moon is at 1 degree in a test-match chart, we can allow all aspects it makes before leaving that sign, 29 degrees later. But suppose the Moon is already at 29 degrees?'

'The rule is:

THE END OF THE SIGN IS THE LIMIT FOR ASPECTS

Do not consider aspects that demand the Moon crosses into the next sign. In a football match, for example, if the Moon is at 28 degrees, we have only 2 degrees of travel. It doesn't carry into the next sign – even if you like the look of the aspect it would make there. But experience suggests that we can make an exception for first-class cricket matches, because of the length of time these games take, which is far in excess of other sports. So if, and only if, the Moon is at a very late degree in the chart for a test or county cricket match, we can allow it into its next sign.'

'How do we judge these aspects, Master? Trine good; opposition bad?'

'No. The nature of the aspect doesn't seem to matter. We have our four main significators: Lords 1, 7, 10 and 4. Whichever of these is the Moon's last aspect over its range wins.

MOON'S FINAL ASPECT WINS
BODILY CONJUNCTIONS ARE USUALLY FINAL

Let's say we're judging a football chart. The Moon makes an immediate square to Lord 10, then an opposition to Lord 7 after travelling 4½ degrees. The final aspect is to Lord 7, one of the underdog's significators: underdog wins.'

'Even though it's an opposition?'

'Even though it's an opposition.'

'What about that first aspect to Lord 10? Does that show the favourites taking an early lead?'

'It can show them having an early advantage, yes. This isn't always translated from pitch to scoreboard, but often is.'

'And what if the Moon made that immediate aspect to Lord 10, then did nothing else? Would that show the favourite winning?'

'Yes.'

'And if it made an immediate conjunction with Lord 10 and then went on to oppose Lord 7, I would ignore that opposition to Lord 7?'

'Yes, don't take the Moon past a conjunction. Treat the conjunction as if it were the final aspect.'

'What about those little animals?'

'They're very important, especially if by conjunction or opposition. Other aspects to antiscia are less reliable, but seem to work if there is nothing else to over-rule them.'

'And the Moon's conjunctions to antiscia are final too?'

'No. That's why I said it is bodily conjunctions that are usually final. Conjunctions by antiscion usually aren't, at least in games where the Moon has its usual range of 5 or 6 degrees. We can take the Moon beyond them. But if we have to move the Moon further than 5 or 6 degrees to reach an antiscial conjunction, it seems so glad to have got there that it gives up and doesn't go any further. This happens mainly in cricket matches, where we can move the Moon over a much greater range. You could say that long-range antiscial conjunctions are final, short-range ones aren't.'

'Now, Master, we are looking at aspects from the Moon to the rulers of our four key houses. But what if the Moon is the ruler of one of these houses?'

'This is a nuisance. I find sulking an appropriate response, but unfortunately that doesn't change anything. The Moon is of such importance in these charts that this confusion of roles is most unhelpful. I suggest:

* If Moon is Lord 1 or Lord 7, keep Moon as the flow of events; use Moon's dispositor as ruler of that house.
* If Moon is Lord 10 or Lord 4, keep Moon as the flow of events; manage without a ruler for that house.

So if the chart has Cancer rising and the Moon is in Scorpio, look at the Moon's aspects, letting Mars stand in as Lord 1.'

I gripped my stick, ready for his next question. He asked it anyway: 'But what if the Moon was in Scorpio and Mars were, say, Lord 10?'

'Too many questions, my boy! Are you a Virgo? If that were the case, we would prioritise: make Mars Lord 1 and manage without Lord 10. Such adaptions are not ideal; as always, we do what we can. I am rarely confident in judgement of one of these charts when Cancer either rises or sets: the dual role of the Moon causes confusion. But if sometimes we bump into our limitations, that is no bad thing.'

'Is that everything about aspects, Master?'

'No. The Moon's aspects are very important; so are **aspects to Fortuna**. These are a little more complicated. Keep the Part of Fortune still, of course: she doesn't move; things come to aspect her.

* Moon to conjunct, trine or sextile Fortuna or its antiscion favours the favourites.
* Moon to square or oppose Fortuna or its antiscion favours the underdog.

Keep within the same ranges as before. But, most importantly:

ASPECTS TO FORTUNA OR ITS ANTISCION ARE FINAL.

So if the Moon moves 1 degree before opposing Fortuna we can ignore all other aspects it might make within its range for that sport. Now, to continue:

* Lord 1 to conjunct Fortuna or its antiscion favours the favourites.
* Lord 1 to oppose Fortuna or its antiscion favours the underdogs.
* Lord 7 to conjunct Fortuna or its antiscion favours the underdogs.
* Lord 7 to oppose the antiscion of Fortuna favours the favourites.

Then we have an anomaly. My experience is that:

* Lord 7 to bodily opposition with Fortuna favours the underdogs.

It would seem that this should work the other way round. When you leave this mountainside and begin working with this method on your own, I suggest you keep a careful eye on its behaviour.'

'I will, Master. What about other aspects from Lord 1 or 7 to the Part of Fortune?'

'I would ignore them. They don't seem to work with any degree of reliability.'

'How close do these aspects need to be?'

'Keep to a limit of around 5 degrees. But because we're not talking about the Moon now, it is most important that you

MAKE SURE THE ASPECT ACTUALLY HAPPENS.

If the planet turns retrograde before it reaches Fortuna, there is no aspect. Similarly with other prohibitions: if Lord 1 aspects another planet before it reaches Fortuna, the aspect to Fortuna doesn't count. That interfering planet has prohibited it.'

'And aspects from Lord 4 or 10 to Fortuna?'

'These don't seem strong enough to decide a contest on their own. If you have mixed testimonies, you can throw them in to support one side or the other, following the same principles as with Lords 1 and 7. Otherwise ignore them.'

'Let's get this straight, Master. When we are looking at house placement we concern ourselves only with the antiscion of Fortuna, ignoring its bodily placement. When we are looking at aspects, we are concerned with both its body and its antiscion.'

'That's right. We must also take notice of the dispositor of Fortuna.'

'You mean the ruler of the sign the Part of Fortune is in?'

'Yes.

* Its dispositor applying to conjunct Fortuna favours the favourites.
* Its dispositor applying to oppose Fortuna favours the underdogs.'

He was opening his mouth, but I answered before he could frame his question: 'If the dispositor of Fortuna is also Lord 10 or Lord 4, give priority to its role as dispositor of Fortuna. If it is also Lord 1, Lord 7, or the Moon, forget its role as dispositor of Fortuna.'

He was beginning to look as if the passage of information through his ears was causing fatigue. 'Don't worry, my boy,' I reassured him, 'we're almost done. Only a few **miscellaneous points** now. I told you to disregard accidental dignities and debilities. There are a couple of exceptions to that rule:

* North Node good; South Node bad.
* Combustion is destructive.

The house placement of the **Nodes** doesn't seem significant, so for instance the North Node on the Ascendant doesn't favour the favourites. But significators falling on the Nodes will be helped or harmed. This is a powerful testimony. In this context, Fortuna can be taken as belonging to the favourite: Fortuna on the North Node helps the favourite; on the South Node it helps the underdog. Conjunctions only, within a couple of degrees at most.'

'And the Moon?'

'That doesn't belong to either side, so its falling on one of the Nodes has no effect.'

'What about **cazimi**? That is usually most strengthening.'

'Not here. A planet cazimi – within 17′ of the Sun – is said to be like a man raised up to sit beside the king. I suspect that it has no effect here because within this context there is no king: we have just our two protagonists wrestling in the mud. No king can reach down to raise one of them up. **Combustion** must be kept much tighter than usual. We can say that any significator within 2 degrees of the Sun is harmed.'

'So Fortuna combust is good news for the underdogs; the Moon combust means nothing?'

'Yes.'

'Are planets weakened by being **retrograde**?'

'In these charts, it seems not. Though retrogradation will, of course, affect which aspects they are able to make, so it cannot be totally ignored.'

'What about **fixed stars**, Master?'

'This level of astrology seems beneath them. Even Regulus, the star most likely to confer victory, has no apparent effect here. But the outer planets are worth noting.'

He raised an eyebrow, evidently wondering if the rarefied air at this altitude had affected my thinking. 'I did tell you we are at the bottom of the astrological food-chain here! **Pluto** has a powerful destructive effect if placed directly on a relevant cusp. If conjunct or opposing Fortuna, or the antiscion or the dispositor of Fortuna, this favours the underdog. In fact, Pluto seems to hold some kind of grudge against favourites: he's much less inclined to work his malice on the under-dog. Even a placement on the 2nd cusp harms the favourites.'

He stared hard at me, trying to work out if I was pulling his leg. I assured him I was not. 'I have judged many of these charts on the placement of Pluto alone. And judged them accurately, mark you.'

'OK, Master,' he continued, trying to suppress a grin, 'so what about **Neptune** and **Uranus**?'

'I've not noticed Neptune doing anything with any consistency. It may be that it too doesn't much like the favourites, so you could keep an eye on it in the charts that you do. Uranus too seems inconsistent, but if applying immediately to the MC it strongly favours the favourites, as also if it conjuncts Fortuna. Opposing Fortuna, it favours the underdog.'

'I suppose all these outer planet contacts must be very close?'

'Very. A degree or so away at most. Finally, we come to **Saturn**. Unless it is busy being Lord 1 or Lord 7, it seems to work as a malefic, afflicting whatever it touches. This will to nastiness seems to take priority over other roles it might have, such as Lord 10.'

'You said "finally", Master.'

'Yes, lad, we're done. Come, let's rouse these creatures and head back to the cave. Then you can make a fire and cook us some lunch.' After some thorough prodding, Britney staggered to her feet. Had she hands, she would have been rubbing her eyes. Sedna too had dropped off, lulled as this flow of testimony trickled past like a stream.

After we had walked for some time in silence, the boy asked me, 'Weighing these testimonies will show us who wins and who loses. But in many of your predictions in print and on TV you have not only forecast the winner, but also the correct score. How do I do that, oh Master?'

I laughed. 'I am giving you the Moon, my lad, and still you want the stars! Predicting the score is not an exact science. At best, it is no more than an educated guess. But, as I have shown, that guess can often be educated enough to prove correct.'

'Can we do this with any sport?'

'No. I have done it only with football. It may be possible with other low-scoring sports, but certainly not with basketball, other codes of football, cricket, and suchlike. The numbers are too high and there is too much variation in them. For a football team to score four goals is unusual; to score six is rare. So we have a limited range of choices. However are we supposed to tell the difference between 79 points and 80 points? How, for that matter, are we supposed to find the number 80 in our chart?'

'But I've heard people saying they can predict basketball and US football scores.'

'And I've seen people playing air-guitar. The absence of reality makes playing so much easier.'

'Tell me the method, Master.'

'As a rough guide, we can say the more testimonies there are the more goals there will be. This is not a simple equation: 2 testimonies = 2 goals. It is a rough guide, and no more than that. So if there is no testimony in favour of one team, that team is unlikely to score. If there are lots of testimonies for the other team, they are likely to score a lot.'

'So we could predict a 6-0 victory!'

'You might, my boy. I would not. A 6-0 victory is possible, and very spectacular it would look if you had predicted it. But with the tools at our disposal it would be no more than foolishness to make such a prediction. 4-0 is a big victory. 6-0 is a big victory. We do not have the tools to distinguish between them – and 6-0 is most unlikely to happen.'

He looked disappointed. I continued, 'Remember what William Lilly so often said: *Combine discretion with art.*[20] To put it another way: *Bear in mind the reality of the situation.* You are not playing air-guitar! In most football matches, the losing side will not score more than one goal. In most matches the winners will score only one or two goals more than the losers. Better to work within these parameters and get things right, at the risk of missing the occasional spectacular hit, than to go chasing the spectacular. That doesn't often happen: that's why it's spectacular.'

'And draws?'

'On the same principle. If testimonies look balanced, we can predict the draw. The number of testimonies will allow us a cautious shot at the number of goals. We'll take a look at a typical goalless-draw chart later. They have a gridlocked appearance, with nothing whatever happening, that you will soon come to recognise.'

By now we had reached the cave, so I set him to work while I spent time rebalancing my inner equilibrium. He woke me for lunch, and as we ate he asked, checking, 'This method works for all sports matches, Master?'

'No. It works with any sport on which I've tried it – and that is a lot of sports. But it is not suited to the run-of-the-mill. Consider the start of a snooker tournament, for instance: we might have a dozen games taking place within the same room, all beginning at the same time. So they all have the same chart. Perhaps in theory it might be possible to pick the astrological bones out of that lot, but I have no idea how we might go about doing so. But wait till the final, and this method will give you the winner.'

'So it only works for finals?'

'No. But that is where it works best. For predicting the result of finals – the Super Bowl, the Aussie Open, the Champions' League final, or the final of your pub's darts tournament – it performs excellently. From that peak of excellence there is a falling away as matches become more commonplace. At 3 o'clock on a Saturday afternoon there will be forty or more professional football matches kicking off in England. England is bigger than that snooker hall, but not much so. Many of these games will have charts that are indistinguishable by anyone who is not a Virgo. This method is quite useless then.'

'What about one-off league games?'

'On a Sunday, there will often be two or three games. The method works tolerably well then. It fulfills our basic desideratum: it gives better results than not using it. On a weekday evening, there will often be only one match played. Then,

---

[20] *Christian Astrology,* passim.

it works rather better, though still not as well as in a true stand-alone, like a final. But on Saturdays the TV schedules often insist on one game kicking off around noon, another at 5.15. It seems not to work for these. It is almost as if these games somehow ought to be kicking off at 3 o'clock, so they sink into the general morass.'

'Maybe it doesn't work so well with these games because they can end in a draw? They're not like a final, which someone has to win.' I wearily hit him with my stick.

'Draws are a nuisance, yes. But you'll find exactly the same happens in tennis and other sports where there are no draws. Second round at Wimbledon: forget it. Final: it works well.'

'But surely, Master, if there is anything in this method it should work at all levels. Can there be a cut-off point beneath which astrology stops working?'

It was time for a demonstration. I went into the cave and returned with an axe. Handing it to him, I asked him to walk to the spinney to chop down a tree to be stacked for firewood. I let him go some way before whistling to attract his attention. 'You're going to carry the wood back on your shoulders?' I called. 'Take Britney with you.' She muttered something under her breath, clambered reluctantly to her feet and set off to join him.

The Sun was setting by the time he returned, grubby with sweat, followed by Britney, who was piled high with wood and grumbling in gutter Yakkish. Once he had unburdened her, I told him to sit down and extend his right hand. 'That nail needs cutting,' I said, picking up the axe and preparing to swing it. He looked at me in horror. I could see his obedience as a pupil wrestling with his desire for self-preservation. 'Do you understand now?' I asked, putting down the axe. 'That something is a good tool for one purpose does not make it a good tool for every purpose. There is not a cut-off point at which astrology stops working; there is a cut-off point at which this particular method stops being useful, just as we will not judge the events of an individual's life by studying the Jupiter/Saturn conjunctions that are so useful in judging the lives of nations.'

'Yes, Master.'

'It's the same with any technique of prediction. It does what it does. Don't ask it to do what it cannot do. We must come to Astrology as humble supplicants; it is not for us to order her about. And always remember: we don't have to predict everything! That we can predict anything at all is a marvel.'

Worn out by his afternoon of labour, the lad could scarcely keep awake. 'Go feed the antiscia, then sleep, my boy. Bright and early tomorrow we'll start work on some charts.'

Bright and early the next morning we did just that. 'Juventus were hot favourites to win the Champions' League final. Informed opinion thought the only uncertainty was the number of goals by which they would beat Borussia Dortmund. Now, take a look, my boy. What do you see?'

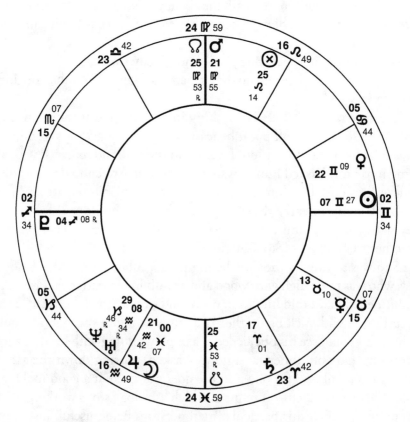

Juventus vs Dortmund, May 28th 1997, 8.30 pm CED, Munich.

He looked at the chart, then at my face, then at my stick, as if fearing to speak. 'Go on, lad. What is it?'

Edging out of easy range, he stammered, 'Master, you said, Pl-Pl-Pluto could be important, and it does grab my attention.'

'Yes, my boy! Pluto only a degree and a half from the Ascendant, and applying retrograde towards it. A powerful testimony of the favourites losing.' He beamed in relief.

'What else?'

He studied his checklist carefully. 'The North Node is right on the MC, but you said that isn't significant. And Mars applies to the MC, but Mars doesn't seem to have a role in this chart.'

'Quite right. Mars isn't one of our significators.'

'The Sun is in the 7th, and the Sun is dispositor of the Part of Fortune. That might favour the underdogs.'

'Well spotted. But it's a long way from the cusp. Too far to be of importance.'

'Master, I'm puzzled. Lord 1 is Jupiter, Lord 7 is Mercury. But Lord 10, which is also for the favourites, is Mercury and Lord 4 Jupiter. What do I do?'

'As so often, the chart is not what we might desire. We must make do. Priority must be given to Lords 1 and 7, which are our main significators. So here we have to manage without Lords 10 and 4.'

'Thank you, Master. Now I must check what the Moon is doing. The only aspect I can see is a sextile to the antiscion of Fortuna, which is at 4 Taurus.'

'Yes. A sextile by antiscion is not strong, but it is worth noting. It can guide any attempt we might make to predict the score, and if we have no other testimony it could even sway the result.'

'I must look to see what our main significators are doing. Oh, look! Jupiter, Lord 1, applies to oppose Fortuna!'

'Good. So we have two powerful testimonies in favour of the underdogs, one minor testimony for the favourites. To the astonishment of the so-called experts, Dortmund won 3-1. That sextile was evidently enough to give the favourites one goal.'

'Can we do another, Master?'

'Of course. In this match Scotland were expected to beat Wales. What do you make of this?'

'Lord 1 stands for Scotland. It is in the 10th house, but too far from the cusp for this to be significant.'

'Good, my boy.'

'It is close to the North Node. That must be good for the favourites.'

'Maybe. I'd think this too far off to be of major importance.'

'Lord 7 applies to square Lord 1, but you said that isn't important. Before that it trines Lord 4, but I don't suppose that is important either.'

'Quite right. What about the Moon?'

'The Moon goes immediately to sextile Saturn. Saturn acts as a malefic...'

'But the Moon's role is as the flow of events, so we don't know which team Saturn is being malefic to.'

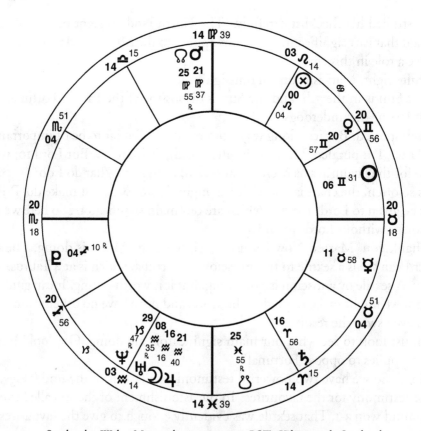

Scotland vs Wales, May 27th 1997, 8.00 pm BST, Kilmarnock, Scotland.

'Then to trine Venus, Lord 7, which favours the underdogs. Its final aspect is the conjunction to Jupiter, Lord 4. I can't see anything else, Master. Wales must win.'

'And so they did. No testimony for the favourites. The important thing is the Moon's final aspect. Wales won 1-0.'

'Look at this one. It is the goalless-draw chart I spoke about. It's typical of the beasts. Tell me what you see.'

With a great deal of huffing, humming, biting of his thumb and scratching of his ear he worked through his checklist of testimonies. 'I can't see anything, Master,' he at last announced. 'Not by placement; not by aspect. There's absolutely nothing happening here.'

'You see what I mean? This was not a mere goalless draw, but the goalless draw of goalless draws – a candidate for the most boring football match ever played. Marseille and Red Star Belgrade had won through to the final of the European

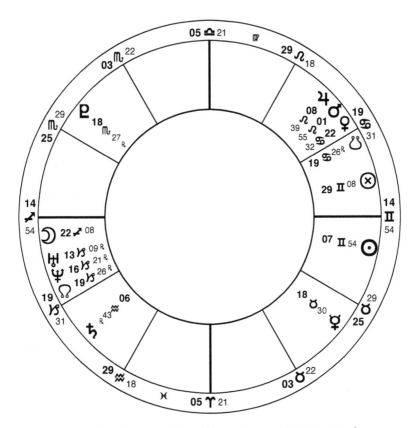

Marseille vs Red Star, May 29th 1991, 8.45 pm CED, Bari, Italy.

Cup playing thrilling attacking football. Aficionados looked forward to a game filled with skill and spectacle. Unfortunately, the coach of the underdogs, Red Star, had decided, "We could not beat Marseille unless they made a mistake, so I told my players to be patient and wait for penalties". They duly stifled the game. But dull though it was, someone had to win. Go back to the chart, boy. Who won?'

'OK, Master. I know it was a goalless draw. So it must have gone to extra time or penalties. I can allow the Moon to move a bit further than usual.'

'And what do you see?'

'Master, it opposes Fortuna in 7 degrees!'

'Yes. The favourites must lose. Red Star's shameful policy paid off. 7 degrees is the absolute limit of motion we can afford the Moon in a football match, so victory must come on penalties. And so it proved.'

'You predicted this, Master?'

'Oh, no! 1991? That was long before I developed this method. A test that it works is that we can project it back into the past, using it on games like this. Here's another. Tell me what you see.'

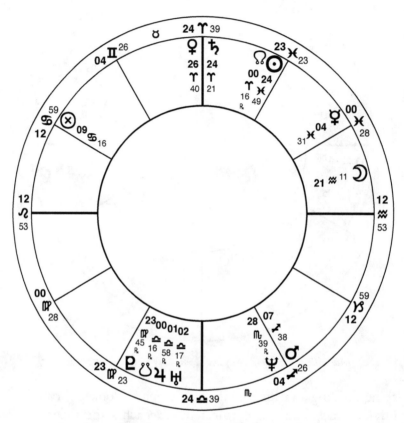

Swindon vs Arsenal, March 15th 1969, 3.00 pm BST, London.

'The placements close to the angles catch my eye, Master. Lord 4 is just inside the 10th house.'

'Meaning?'

'Lord 4 is for the underdogs, so this is an advantage to the favourites. But Lord 7 applies immediately to the 10th cusp. This must be a positive for the underdogs, and a much stronger testimony than Lord 4 in the 10th, because it is so much closer.'

Sometimes I could have reached out and embraced the lad, my heart brim full with joy at what he had learned. Such behaviour would be unbecoming of a

Master Astrologer, so I thumped him affectionately around the head with my stick. He could see that I was pleased with him.

'Now I must look at the Moon's movement,' he continued. 'It sextiles Lord 7 after 3 degrees. Then it sextiles Lord 4 having moved just over 5 degrees. Was extra time possible in this game?'

'Yes.'

'OK. So I judge that the underdogs won in extra time, with the favourites scoring at least one goal, on the basis of that Lord 4 placement.'

'And so it proved, my boy. Swindon, a small club from the third tier of English football, humbled the mighty Arsenal, winning 3-1 after extra time.'

He looked suitably pleased with himself, but after a few moments of self-congratulation and much affectionate stroking of Sedna he asked, 'Master, I fear that if ever I am to teach these methods to students of my own, I may have to venture

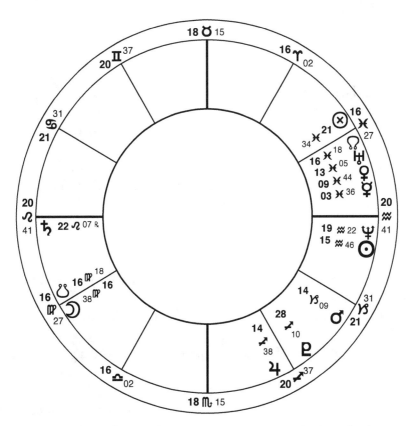

Super Bowl, February 4th 2007, 6.25 pm EST, Miami Gardens, Florida.

among the infidels, whose lives are held in thrall to that dark idol, Gridiron. Could we look at some American football charts, please?'

'Of course. You must be well prepared for that eventuality. This chart is of the 2007 Super Bowl. Indianapolis Colts were favourites to beat the Chicago Bears. Look at your worksheet and tell me what you think.'

'I see Lord 7 just inside the 1st house. That puts the underdogs in a very bad situation. But it's retrograde and applying to the cusp.'

'No matter: that still doesn't give it any power over that cusp. It is its position, trapped inside the house, that is the important thing. It may be banging on the cell door, but it is still in prison. What else do you see?'

'Lord 1 applies to the 7th cusp. Or is that too far, Master?'

'Yes. It is 5 degrees from the cusp. Much too far to concern us. Are there any aspects?'

He thought for a while. 'The Moon will oppose Fortuna. That's good for the Bears. That's all I can see, Master. One strong testimony for each team. So who wins?'

'This terrible house placement must outweigh anything else. The favourites won. A strong house placement, especially of Lord 1 or 7, will usually outweigh anything else. Here's another: a game from 1998, where Kansas City, with their awesome home record, were seen as certainties to see off Pittsburgh.'

'I see the Moon goes to sextile Lord 7, and then to sextile Lord 1. That would appear to help the favourites.'

'Look at the distance to Lord 1, though: almost 6 degrees. That's too far for American football. So the Moon's final aspect within range is to Lord 7.'

'But I thought American football matches lasted forever.'

'It only seems like that, my boy. It can indeed be a long time from kick-off to the final whistle, but at four periods of fifteen minutes, it is one of the shortest forms of football, so the Moon has a shorter range.'

'Mercury, which is Lord 1, goes to square Fortuna. But you said such aspects are too unreliable for use.'

'Yes, they seem able to go either way. What else? Don't forget those little animals.'

'Aha!' His eyes gleamed. 'I see what you mean. First, Lord 4 goes to oppose the antiscion of Fortuna. From what you said about aspects of Lords 1 and 7 to Fortuna, I suppose that should favour the favourites.'

'Maybe. I'd be very cautious with it, though. A conjunction would be important, but, at most, aspects from Lords 4 and 10 to Fortuna are far weaker than

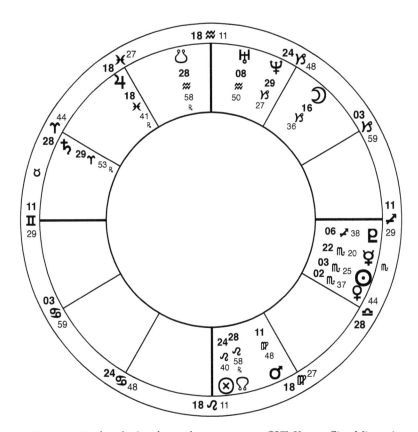

Kansas vs Pittsburgh, October 26th 1998, 7.20 pm CST, Kansas City, Missouri.

those from Lords 1 and 7. Think again, though. The Sun has another role here, besides being Lord 4.'

He thought again, until he realised, 'It's the dispositor of Fortuna! So the dispositor of Fortuna goes to oppose Fortuna by antiscion. That favours the underdogs.'

'Yes. Remember what I told you: if the dispositor of Fortuna is also Lord 10 or Lord 4, we must give priority to its role as dispositor of Fortuna.'

'Is that everything, Master?'

'There's more. Look at the Moon.'

'Yes! The antiscion of the Moon is at 13.24 Sagittarius, just inside the 7th house. The underdogs have control of the game.'

'And so it proved. Pittsburgh won. Another?'

'Yes, please, Master.'

'Let's go back into history. What do you make of this one?'

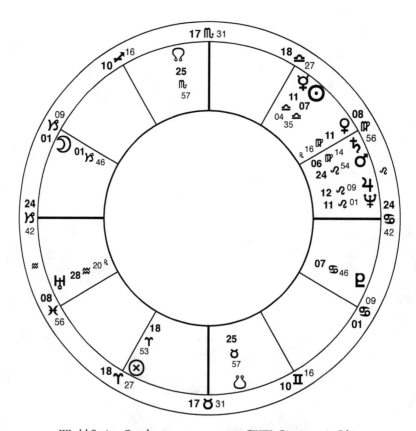

World Series, October 1st 1919, 3.00 pm CWT, Cincinnati, Ohio.

'There's no obvious testimony by house placement. The Moon goes to trine Lord 1 – but as the Moon is Lord 7 I don't think I can count that as significant.'

'That's correct. We can't keep the Moon as the flow of events here, using its dispositor as Lord 7, because its dispositor is Lord 1. We're stymied.'

'I'd better check those little animals again. Look, Master! Lord 4 makes an immediate conjunction with the antiscion of Fortuna. Nothing else happening. The favourites must lose.'

'And so they did. This is the first game of the 1919 World Series. The famous "Black Sox" scandal, where the Chicago White Sox were bribed to throw the series to the Cincinnati Reds. You must have heard the phrase "Say it ain't so, Joe", said to have been a small boy's plea to his tarnished hero, Shoeless Joe Jackson. We wouldn't usually look any further than the result, but the position of Lord 2, the favourites' money, is interesting here. Right on the IC by antiscion, pointing its connection with the underdogs' success, close enough to Neptune to suggest something fishy going on, and on the fixed star Acubens. That's the brightest star in the constellation of Cancer. As such it is associated with spontaneous desires – financial ones in this case – and is, according to the authority on fixed stars, Vivian Robson, associated with malevolence, liars and criminals.'[21]

'You mean this stuff works, Master?' I cuffed him around the ears as I drew up another chart for him to study. 'It's the Super Bowl again. St Louis Rams were favourites to beat Tennessee Titans. What do you see?'

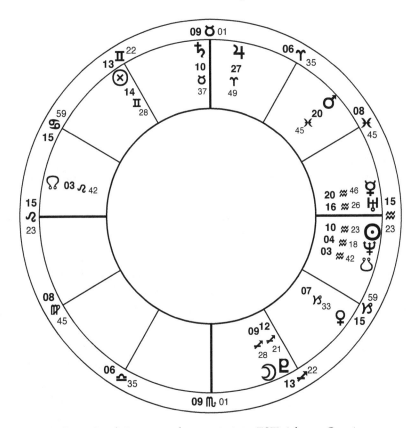

Super Bowl, January 30th 2000, 6.26 pm EST, Atlanta, Georgia.

'Immediate testimony, Master: Lord 7 tucked just inside the 10th cusp. It would need a lot to outweigh this evidence that the favourites win.'

'Yes, you're quite right. It is good to cultivate an eye for the immediate

21 Robson, op. cit. p. 116.

evidence – the things that are jumping up and down in the chart shouting "Look at me! Look at me!" But we must not be content with these alone. We must check for less obvious things, too. I don't know how much time it is worth spending on these charts; I think but little. But they do always demand more than a glance.'

'Right, Master. Down to work.' This, of course, occasioned a deal of grunting and scratching to demonstrate that thought processes were taking place. 'The Moon goes to sextile Lord 1. That's good for the favourites. Then to conjunct Pluto. What does that mean, Master?'

'Nothing much. If it were an immediate conjunction of Lord 1 to Pluto, that might be bad news for the favourites, but I've not noticed any significance in a Moon conjunction. Then what?'

'After exactly 5 degrees it opposes Fortuna. That's a strong testimony for the underdog.'

'So who wins?'

'You told me that it takes an awful lot to outweigh a powerful testimony by house placement. Tucked so closely inside the 10th house, this placement of Lord 7 is very powerful. And 5 degrees is probably too far for the Moon to travel in American football. The favourites must win.'

'And so they did, my boy. And so they did. Now compare this chart, which is another Super Bowl. The New England Patriots were favoured to beat the Carolina Panthers. Who wins?'

'The first thing I see is Lord 10 right on the 10th cusp. This is such a strong testimony for the favourites. Must I really look further, Master?'

My stick gave him my answer. 'OK, Master. Lord 1 is in the 7th house. But much too far from the cusp for that to be significant.'

'Good, my boy!'

'The Moon conjuncts the antiscion of Saturn. That must favour the underdogs.'

Again my stick fell into action. 'Look, boy, look! Where is the antiscion of Saturn?'

Scratching in the dust of the mountain-side he did the sum: 'Saturn is at 7.22 Cancer.

The antiscion of anything in Cancer is in Gemini. To find out which degree of Gemini I must subtract those 7.22 degrees from 30. To simplify the arithmetic I can call 30 degrees 29.60 degrees.

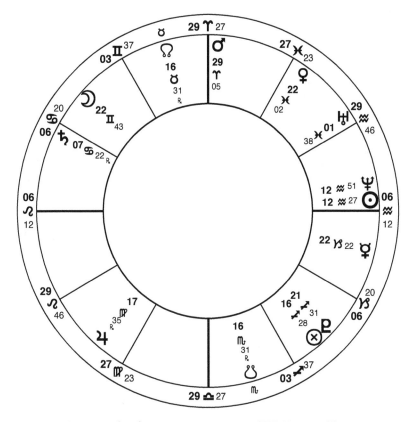

Super Bowl, February 1st 2004, 5.25 pm CST, Houston, Texas.

So: 29.60

         7.22 −

      $\overline{22.38}$

So the antiscion of Saturn at 7.22 Cancer falls at 22.38 Gemini.'

    'Yes. So?'

    'Yes, Master. The Moon is at 22.43 Gemini. So it is already separating from the conjunction with the antiscion of Saturn. This is past. It's not relevant.'

    'So it is. Alas for the underdogs, it seems: had the game started a short time earlier, we might have judged that the favourites would lose. But that is in the magic world of *What if,* where anything can happen. We are interested only in the world of *What is.* That is all that we have to work with. All that we have to live with.'

'So the only important testimony is Lord 10 on the 10th cusp. Favourites win.'
'And so it proved, my boy. Here's another.'

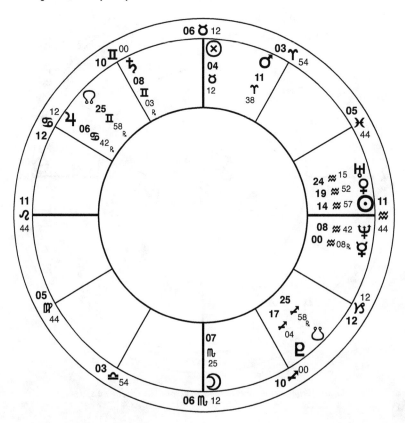

Super Bowl, February 3rd 2002, 5.20 pm CST, New Orleans, Louisiana.

'Oh, Master, there's lots of placements here! Fortuna is on the MC, though you said that the bodily placement of Fortuna isn't important.'

'Good. You must check where its antiscion falls, though.'

'Fortuna is at 4.12 Taurus, so its antiscion is at 25.48 Leo. Floating around in the middle of the first house: no significance in that. But it's opposed by Uranus. Is this close enough to matter?'

'A degree and a half away: that's stretching things a little, but it may favour the underdogs.'

'Then we have Lord 1 just inside the 7th house. That's a clear testimony for the underdogs.'

'3 degrees inside the house, so we're close to the limits of what is worth noting. But I think we can mark this one up.'

'Then there's the Moon so close inside the 4th cusp. That must favour the underdogs.'

'Yes, a very strong testimony. Is there anything else – an aspect, perhaps?'

He scoured the chart before announcing, 'Yes! The Moon goes to conjunct the antiscion of Venus, Lord 10, at 10.08 Scorpio. That's one for the favourites.'

'But the overwhelming verdict is for the underdogs, especially with that powerful Moon placement. The New England Patriots beat the St Louis Rams in one of the biggest surprises in the history of the Super Bowl.'

'Master, I know nothing about American football. Is that a problem? Isn't a knowledge of the sport helpful?'

'Beyond an awareness of the most basic points, such as whether a draw is a possible result or if the game must produce a winner, I would say not. In fact, that knowledge can be a hindrance. I would often judge a chart and then think "No, that result's not possible. So-and-so is bound to win." Eventually I had to admit that the stars know a lot more about sport than I do. My supposedly expert knowledge looked very threadbare.'

'That's reassuring, Master!'

'Let's have a look at some other sports. Compare the charts on the next page. What is the significant difference between them?'

'They're almost identical, Master. They must be cast for the same time but different places.'

'Yes. They were for the semi-finals of the NatWest Trophy, a one-day cricket competition. In the Manchester game, Lancashire were favoured to beat Yorkshire. In London, Surrey were favourites to beat Essex. So: what's the big difference between them?'

'It's Mars, Master. In the Manchester chart it is inside the 10th house; in the London chart it is sitting on the cusp of the 10th house.'

'Good. So what does this tell us?'

'Mars is Lord 7, main significator of the underdogs. Such a powerful testimony, a testimony by placement, will be pivotal. In London, Lord 7 dominates the 10th house: the underdogs must win. In Manchester, it is trapped inside the 10th house: the underdogs must lose.'

'And so it proved, my boy. You see how simple these charts can be?'

'Yes, Master. It's awesome! We can tell so much from such a slight difference in the placement of one planet.'

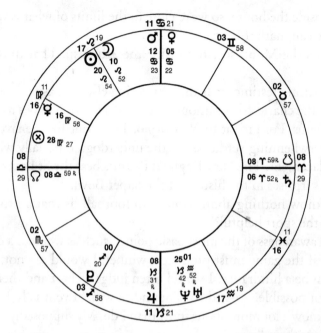

NatWest semi-final, August 13th 1996, 10.30 am BST, Manchester.

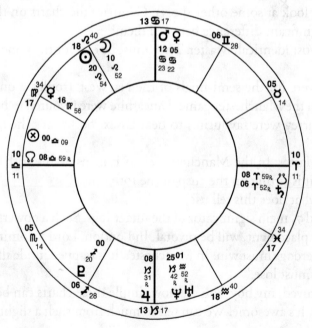

NatWest semi-final, August 13th 1996, 10.30 am BST, London.

'Here's a tennis chart. It's the men's final at the French Open. The biggest problem with predicting tennis, or for that matter boxing, is knowing when the contest will start. We usually don't know that until it has actually started. You see why we need a quick, simple system!'

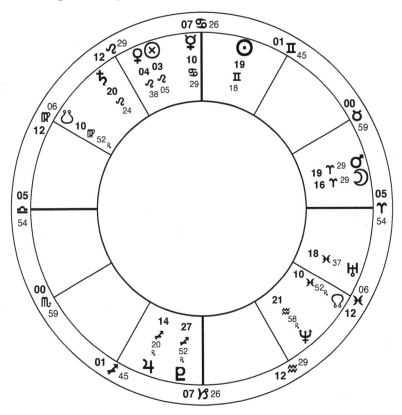

French Open, men's final, June 10th 2007, 3.09 pm CED, Paris.

'Right, Master. I see Mercury very prominent, close inside the 10th house. But Mercury doesn't seem to have a role in this chart, so I can ignore it.'

'Good. Don't feel obliged to drag it in just because it's there.'

'The Moon makes an immediate conjunction to Lord 7, then goes on to trine Lord 4. That's a strong testimony for the underdog. I can't see anything else. The favourite loses.'

'That's a strong testimony, yes. Conjunctions are usually a cut-off point in the Moon's aspects, so we needn't take it beyond that. We can ignore its aspect to Saturn. We can also ignore its first aspect, which is the sextile to the Sun. The Sun is the dispositor of Fortuna, so it's possible this sextile is a minor testimony for the favourite, but I wouldn't place much value on it. But look again. You're missing something important.'

'Lord 1 is conjunct Fortuna. But that's separating, so that's not relevant.' He lapsed into silence.

'Look at Lord 7. And remember those little animals.'

'Ah! The antiscion of Mars is at 10.31 Virgo, right on the South Node. That's an affliction.'

'Yes. And as I told you, it's a serious affliction. Quite powerful enough to overwhelm the evidence of the Moon's aspect. With the underdog so debilitated, the favourite must win, and so it proved: Rafael Nadal beat Roger Federer.'

'What about the movement here? Is the antiscion applying to the South Node, or the South Node applying to it? In that masterful work *The Horary Textbook* we're told not to try moving antiscia at risk of causing lasting damage to our brains.'[22]

'Quite right. Don't move antiscia and don't move the Nodes. We're not concerned with movement here. The South Node is the centre of a small area of nastiness. Being in that area is sufficient; it doesn't matter where the planet is going. Similarly, the North Node is the centre of a small area of niceness.'

'More, please, Master.'

How pleasing was this enthusiasm! 'Try this one. It's for a cricket test match.'

'Again, there is an obvious placement: the Sun on the 10th cusp. But I can't see that the Sun has a role here.'

'Good. It doesn't.'

'Then look at Neptune, applying retrograde to the 7th cusp. It's so close that this might be important. What does it mean, Master?'

'Your guess is as good as mine. You're young, boy: you will have plenty of opportunity to observe this planet and study its wily ways. As I told you, I've not noticed it doing anything with any consistency.'

'Then there's Lord 10, Mercury, applying to conjunct Uranus. What about that?'

'If I had to take a position on this I'd say it favoured the underdogs. But I really don't know. Again, I haven't observed much consistency in the action of Uranus.'

'I must say, Master,' he began, crawling on all fours to take shelter behind Britney's slumbering form, 'for a Master Astrologer there's a lot you don't know.'

'So there is. Vast amounts. From your low perspective, you cannot even imagine

[22] p. 104.

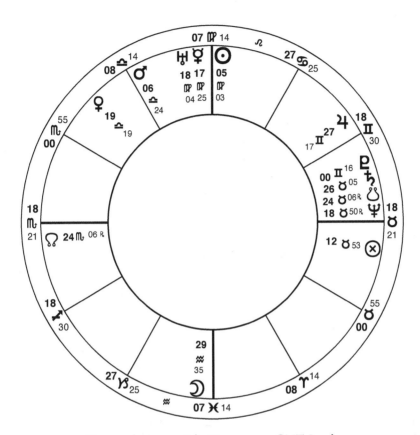

Test match, August 28th 1882, 12.10 pm GMT, London.

the vistas of ignorance that I survey. I used to have a friend once. He was very tall, yet his head came nowhere near the sky.'

I thought about thumping him for his impertinence, but didn't want to wake the yak. It would wait. From his hiding-place he continued, 'By placement, there's nothing else that I can see. The Moon is too far from the 4th cusp for that to count.'

'Yes, so far as placement is concerned, it's where the planet *is* that matters, not where it's going to.'

'I can't see any relevant aspects, Master. With the Moon so late in its sign there isn't much chance of that doing anything.'

'Remember what I told you: this is the chart for a cricket test match. So you can take the Moon into its next sign. And remember those...'

'Little animals. Yes, Master, I remember them. Let me see. The antiscion of

Lord 1 is at 23.36 Pisces. The Moon will eventually conjunct it. But the antiscion of Lord 7 is at 10.41 Pisces. The Moon conjuncts that first.'

'And what did I tell you about conjunctions?'

'They are usually final, Master. But this is an antiscial conjunction. If the Moon had moved only a few degrees to make it, it would not have been final, but at this distance – over 10 degrees – it is. So it is this first conjunction with Lord 7 that matters here. The favourites lose. Is that right?'

'So it is. This was when a bunch of Australians came to England and had the cheek to beat us at our national game. An obituary was published, lamenting the death of English cricket and saying the body has been cremated and the ashes taken to Australia. England and Australia now compete every couple of years for the possession of these ashes.'

Feeling secure in his hiding-place he giggled, 'So that was a chart you cast early in your career, Master?' I glanced at Sedna, who, once he had subdued his own cackling at this comment, flew up behind the boy and pecked fiercely at the top of his head. That stopped his giggles.

'Let's look at a couple of charts from England's latest attempt to regain those ashes. What do you make of this one? Australia were firm favourites.'

'There's nothing happening by placement here. I'll have to check the aspects.'

'Little animals?'

'OK, Master. Oh, I see: Lord 4 is tightly conjunct Pluto by antiscion. That doesn't look promising for England, the underdogs.'

'What is the Moon doing?'

'It makes an immediate sextile with Lord 7. Does that mean England get off to a good start?'

'Yes. Then what?'

'The Moon goes onto the North Node by antiscion. But the Moon's role here is as the flow of events. I can't see that this conjunction tells us anything, one way or the other.'

'Correct. And then?'

'Well, its final aspect is a square to the antiscion of Lord 1, Jupiter. Jupiter's at 4.24 Sagittarius, so its antiscion is at 25.36 Capricorn. Final aspect is to Lord 1: the favourites win.'

'And so they did. What about this one? It's another match from that same series.'

'Oh, Master – there's a cracking testimony by placement here! Lord 1, Jupiter, just inside the 10th house. Do England stand a chance?'

'Not much of one.

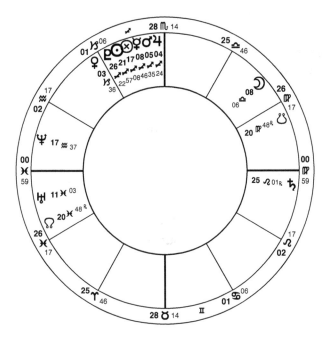

Test match, December 14th 2006, 10.30 am AWST, Perth, Australia.

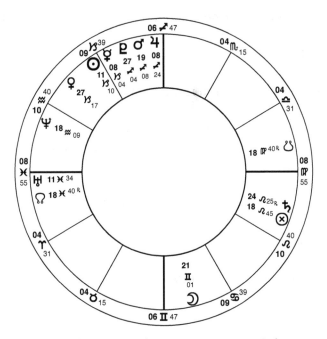

Test match, January 2nd 2007, 10.30 am AEDT, Sydney.

ANY TESTIMONY IN ANY CHART ON ANY SUBJECT CAN BE OVERRULED

but the stronger the testimony the less likely it is that this will happen. This does yell "Aussies will win!" but we must look around the chart to see if anything argues against it.'

'I'll check the aspects, Master. The Moon makes an immediate opposition to the antiscion of Lord 7, which is at 21.56 Sagittarius. This can't be good for the underdogs.'

'Were you asleep when I was talking to you? I told you,' and I beat this out upon his skull in the hope that somehow I might force this information inside it, 'that an aspect even by opposition favours that significator. Moon goes to oppose Lord 7, by antiscion: the underdogs get off to a good start. Then what?'

'The Moon goes to oppose Pluto. But you told me that doesn't mean anything much.'

'Good.'

'And then nothing. The Moon is much too far from the end of its sign to carry into the next sign. I think this chart comes down to the placement of Lord 1. The favourites must win.'

'And so it proved. Even had there not been that strong testimony for Australia, we must always remember the default option. What happens if nothing happens?

THE FAVOURITES WILL WIN IF THERE IS NO EVIDENCE TO THE CONTRARY

That's why they're favourites. You must use your common sense here. If one side in this game is only slightly favoured, it wouldn't need much evidence to judge them losing. If Manchester United were playing your local pub team, we would need something very persuasive in the chart before we would judge against them. I'll say it again:

COMBINE DISCRETION WITH ART.

Have you got that?'

'Yes, oh Master.'

'Now let's have a look at a rugby chart. Bath were hot favourites to beat Newcastle.'

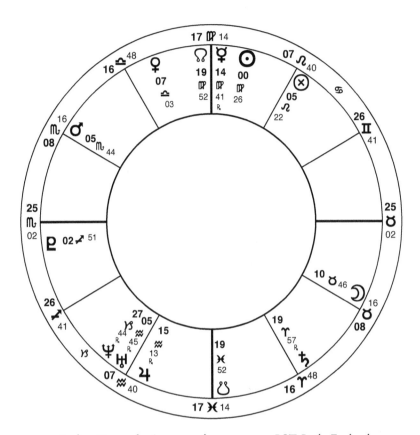

Bath vs Newcastle, August 23rd 1997, 2.15 pm BST, Bath, England.

'By placement, I see Lord 10 close to the 10th cusp. But it's not so close, and it's retrograding away.'

'Yes, this is testimony for the favourites, but not such a strong one.'

'Oh, Master! Those little animals! The antiscion of Fortuna is at 24.38 Taurus, right on the 7th cusp: big testimony in favour of the underdogs.'

'Yes, one of the most powerful possible. Good!'

'Then I must check the aspects. The Moon trines Mercury, which is Lord 10. Then it goes to square Jupiter, Lord 4. That is its last aspect over the 5-degree range. Lord 4 is for the underdogs: Bath must lose.'

'And so it proved, my boy. You're getting the hang of this. Compare these two charts. We're back with football now: the English and the Scottish Cup Finals. They kicked off at the same time, one in London, the other in Glasgow.'

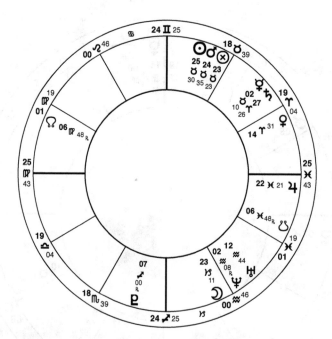

FA Cup Final, May 16th 1998, 3.00 pm BST, London.

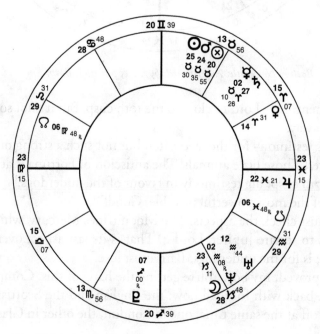

Scottish FA Cup Final, May 16th 1998, 3.00 pm BST, Glasgow.

'They're certainly very similar charts, Master.'

'As we would expect. London and Glasgow aren't so far apart. What do you see?'

'There's a testimony by placement: Lord 7 on the 7th cusp. That looks good for the underdogs.'

'Any thoughts on the comparison between the two charts?'

He scratched his chin. 'It's much closer to the cusp in the Glasgow chart. It's over 3 degrees away in London. Isn't that too far?'

'Yes. So what does that tell you?'

'The underdogs look likely to win in Scotland.'

'So far, yes. What else do you see?'

'There's nothing, other than the Moon's aspects. It goes to trine Fortuna. That's good for the favourites.'

'Are you sure, though? Look again, checking both charts.'

'Oh, Master – the Moon trines Fortuna in the London chart, but in Scotland that trine is already passed. That means in London we have a good testimony for the favourites and nothing for the underdogs; in Glasgow we have a strong testimony for the underdogs and nothing for the favourites.'

'And that's how the games panned out. In London, Arsenal beat Newcastle as expected. In Scotland, Hearts gained a most unexpected victory over Rangers.'

'Did you know the result, though, Master? Isn't it easy to do predictions after the event?'

'I missed that first England/Australia cricket match, but with these, as with so many of the charts I'm showing you, my predictions were either published or televised beforehand.'

We sat in thought for a while, he contemplating the charts I had shown him, me watching the wheeling of an eagle in the clear air above my head. 'These principles do seem very simple,' he said. 'Isn't there more to it than this?'

'There is always more. I was tempted to give you a long list of all the many testimonies that I have seen in one chart or another and thought might have some significance. But this would overcook your brain, bringing confusion rather than enlightenment. I could overwhelm you with that torrent of testimonies, but where would it get you? Most of them would be irrelevant most of the time, and many of them would prove to be plain wrong. Better, I believe, to work with what I'm giving you here: some simple principles. Remember, I have consistently produced results from this. Let what I have told you take you as far as it can, then expand this list judiciously as your own experience guides you.'

'That sounds like you expect me to do some work, Master.'

I staggered back in astonishment, tripping over Britney's outstretched leg and landing with some loss of dignity hard on the ground. A fierce glance at Sedna told him to suppress his cackling. The lad was right. He had stumbled upon the Secret of Secrets; the Major Arcana; the Direct Road to Astrological Enlightenment. 'Yes, dear boy, you are right. You are going to have to do some work. I cannot tell you every answer. Not that I am unwilling: I am striving here to teach you all I can. But teaching is not a packing of the brain with information. I can give you the raw materials, but they must be transformed. Only effort on your part will produce the fierce alchemy that turns what I tell you into something of your own.'

He looked from Sedna to Britney and back again as if hoping that one of them would intercede with me, or would offer to exert the necessary effort on his behalf. Britney, despite my tumbling over her leg, was still soundly sleeping. Sedna returned his pleading gaze coldly. Do not try to out-stare a raven: you will not succeed.

He was disappointed, devastated almost. The magic wand was not quite what he had expected, but was contained only within himself. I had not accepted the boy as my student without seeing a certain potential in him, however. I knew he had the character that would make all the effort that would be required. He pulled himself together, resolving, 'I will do that work, Master, if that alone is what will lead me to mastery of this craft. I want to emulate you. Imagine – in years to come I could be making these predictions on TV! Fame! Fortune!'

I smiled. It was well that he should have a carrot dangling in front of his nose, and if that carrot had some sugar on it, so what? I did not disillusion him about the fame and fortune, but did say, 'TV has given me much of value, my lad. Once one has shared the screen with a troupe of stripping dwarves, it is difficult to be precious about oneself.[23] Or had one's masterful predictions sandwiched between episodes of *Topless Darts*.'[24]

He looked aghast at such lese-majesty. I shook him out of his horror by taking some leaves and drawing charts on them for him to judge by himself. Here they are. All are favourite against underdog; the sports are as listed. The judgements are in Appendix 4.

---

[23] 'The Half Monty', on *Richard Littlejohn - Live and Direct*.
[24] On the cable channel *L!VE TV*.

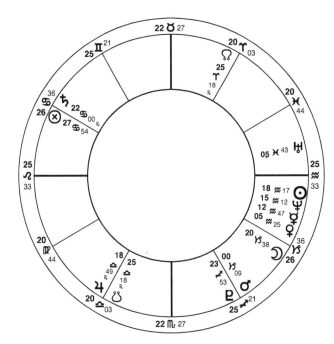

*Test chart 7. American foot-
ball. February 6th 2005, 6.38
pm EST, Jacksonville,
Florida.*

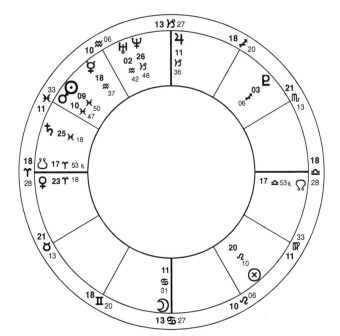

*Test chart 8. One-day
cricket. February 29th 1996,
9.00 am INT, Poona, India.*

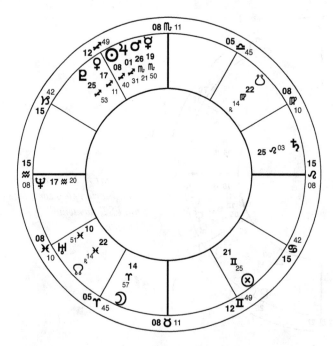

Test chart 9. Cricket test match. December 1st 2006, 11.00 am ACDT, Adelaide, Australia.

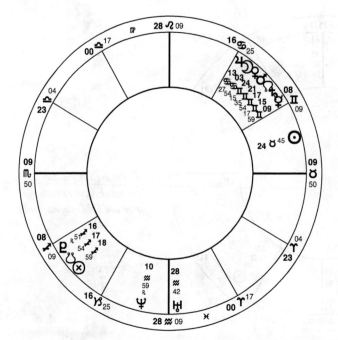

Test chart 10. Football, extra time possible. May 15th 2002, 7.45 pm BST, Glasgow, Scotland.

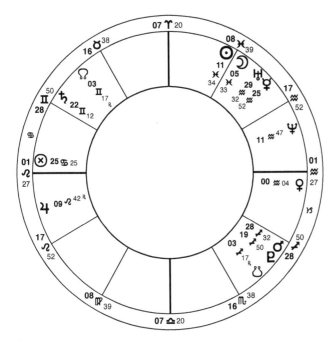

Test chart 11. Football, extra time possible. March 2nd 2003, 2.00 pm GMT, Cardiff, Wales.

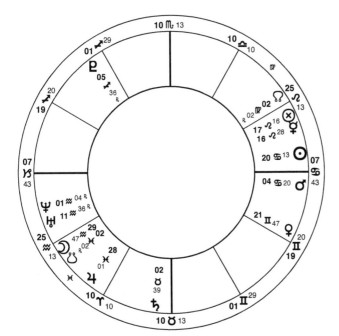

Test chart 12. Football, extra time possible. July 12th 1998, 9.00 pm CED, Paris.

As I rose to walk back to the cave, leaving him to work on these charts, I offered him a final piece of advice, 'Always remember, my lad: if the result doesn't turn out as you have predicted, it isn't your fault. Blame the players, who have failed to stick to the script.' Hearing that, Sedna fluttered onto my shoulder and gave my ear what passes among ravens for a kiss.

INTERLUDE:

BABE RUTH HITS 60 HOME RUNS

When George Ruth signed his first baseball contract, for the Baltimore Orioles, his childlike personality soon had him nicknamed 'Babe'. Had his colleagues studied his birthchart, they could not have found a more suitable name. What else would you call someone with Cancer rising and the Moon in Cancer tucked just inside the Ascendant?

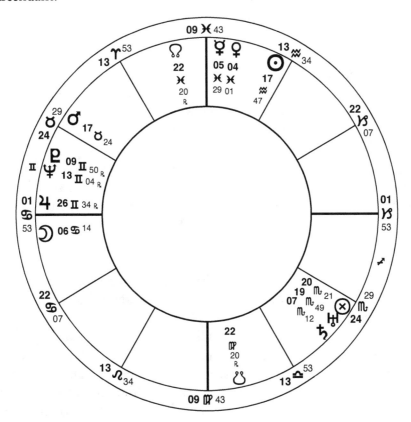

Babe Ruth, February 6th 1895, 1.45 pm EST, Baltimore, Maryland.

A planet in the Ascendant is first choice as Significator of Manner, a title which means exactly what it says: this planet shows how the person behaves. When this planet is also the Lord of the Ascendant, that behaviour runs deep. Being in Cancer, boundaries and discipline will be weak – all the more so when that planet is the Moon. Boundaries will be ignored with all the carelessness of babyhood. For better or for worse: the same man whom Red Sox owner Harry Frazee described as 'one of the most selfish and inconsiderate men ever to put on a baseball uniform,' devoted huge amounts of time and money to his charities for deprived children and was, said teammate Ernie Shore, 'the best-hearted fellow who ever lived; he'd give you the shirt off of his back.' His appetites for food, drink, tobacco, women knew no boundaries – his temper knew but few. But put a man with such an innate ignorance of boundaries, a blindness for 'No Entry' signs, into a sporting arena and he will break records with ease.

If, of course, he has the physical attributes to match this mental aptitude. Otherwise the only records he will break will be for sofa-warming. Ruth's Moon fell directly onto the Jupiter of the previous eclipse chart. Jupiter in its exaltation: that too has no regard for boundaries. It is powerful. It is not finicky and precise. Ruth brought an end to the mercurial precision of 'scientific baseball', where hits were carefully placed between fielders. The Sultan of Swat went out and slugged, harder and farther than anyone believed possible. His slugging percentage for the 1920 season remained unsurpassed for 80 years. Baseball had changed a lot by the time that record was broken.

In his solar return chart for 1919, exalted Jupiter falls exactly on the natal Moon that fell exactly on the exalted Jupiter of the pre-birth eclipse. The Moon, Ascendant ruler in the nativity and hence main significator of Ruth himself, is itself exalted. For good measure, the exalted Venus of the nativity has returned to its natal position. That season, Ruth hit 29 home runs, breaking a record that had stood for 35 years.

The next year he slipped into hyper-drive. These strong connections from the return chart to the nativity were enough for him to add two home runs to the old record. The return chart for 1920 plugs directly into the pre-birth eclipse: he added 25 runs to his own record of 29, hitting 54 homers, and setting that slugging record.

Season followed memorable season until 1925, when Ruth's progressed Moon opposed his natal Sun. William Lilly, writing three hundred years earlier, said such a progression brought with it 'extreme dangers and torments of body and mind...violent and extreme fevers...torments of the belly'.[25] He had by then accu-

---

[25] *Christian Astrology* p. 697.

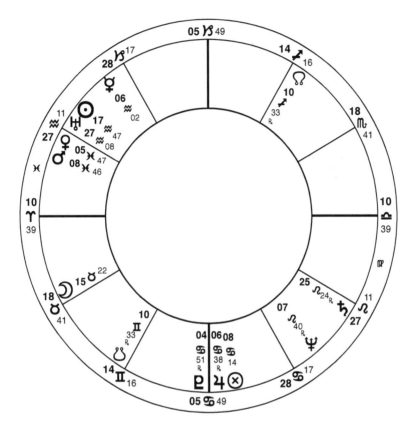

Babe Ruth, Solar Return 1919.

mulated plenty of potential for internal malfunctions. He suffered 'severe stomach cramps and a fever',[26] which worsened into collapse and delirium. An intestinal abscess was diagnosed and operated upon. Unsurprisingly, this was a poor season, his worst while still at his prime. This is confirmed by the solar return's Ascendant falling on the natal South Node, while the return's own South Node falls on his Sun. The return Moon, significator of Ruth himself, is about to leave its own sign of Cancer: strong testimony of life going downhill.

Next season he was back on top, once again the league's best hitter, though susceptible to a drawback of that lack of boundaries: rashness. His failed attempt to steal a base undid a glorious batting display to lose the World Series. It's not often that the final out of a World Series is a caught stealing. But it was in the 1927 season that he again broke his own record for home runs.

[26] http://en.wikipedia.org/wiki/Babe_Ruth

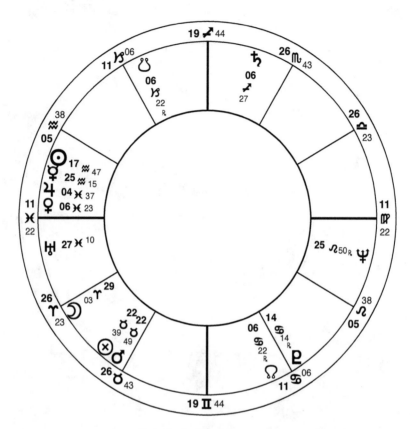

Babe Ruth, Solar Return 1927.

If it were possible to phone out for a solar return as one phones out for a pizza, Ruth's 1927 return is one any sportsman would delightedly order. The return Ascendant picks up his natal Midheaven, which is always a sign of a good year, especially in career matters. Hovering above the Ascendant is Venus, which has returned to its natal position, exactly as it had in his return for 1919, the year he first broke the home-run record. This time, however, it is accompanied by mighty Jupiter, in its own sign and with powerful mutual reception between it and Venus. Jupiter rules both the natal and return 10th house, while Venus rules the natal 5th, so the awesome benefic power of this conjunction targets his career, which was, of course, of a 5th-house nature. The 5th house of the return is emphasised by its cusp picking up the natal Moon, which as the natal Ascendant-ruler signifies Ruth himself, and by the placement of the benefic, expansive North Node. The Node falls exactly on, and therefore expands still further, that natal Moon – which is itself on the exalted, expansive Jupiter of the pre-birth eclipse. There is some expansive stuff going on here! In contrast to the return of 1925, when he was so ill, the Moon here is about to enter the sign of its exaltation: strong testimony of life going uphill, and fast.

As if this wasn't enough, the total solar eclipse of June 29th 1927 fell exactly on his natal Moon. The Bambino slugged 60 home runs, a feat not outdone until 1961, by which time the season was eight games longer.

3

A day at the races

One morning, as I sat contemplating the movement of the celestial spheres with the assistance of an especially fine Tibetan shiraz, he came rushing down the hillside, tumbling head over heels in his haste. 'Master, Master!' he cried, pointing into the valley, 'What's going on down there?'

Sedna whispered the information in my ear. 'It's the 7th day of the 7th New Moon,' I said, 'the day of the village fair.'

'Can we go, Master? Oh, please can we go?'

I decided a holiday would do no harm, and Sedna was flapping up and down with enthusiasm for the idea, but I thought to test him to prove the holiday was deserved. 'Who invented the steam-engine?' I asked.

'William Lilly!' he replied without hesitation.

'You have studied well, my boy. Yes, you shall go to the fair.'

He set to work braiding a garland of mountain flowers to hang around Britney's neck, while I went into the cave to don my Master Astrologer's walking-out gear: a star-emblazoned robe of midnight blue and a pointy hat. Soon we were all ready.

'Do they have yak races, Master? We can enter Britney.' A bellow of leonine ferocity suggested this idea had not met unanimous approval, as the lad fell to the ground clutching his knee in pain. Foolish boy, to stand behind Britney while making a suggestion like that. He was unable to walk, so I helped him onto her back, giving her a stern look lest she have further ideas for teaching him manners.

We set off along the path into the valley, him clinging to Britney's coat and Sedna riding noisily on my shoulder as I walked beside them. There were indeed yak races at the fair. His eyes lit up. 'Can we predict the winners, Master? Show me how to do that.'

'There are many methods for picking winners astrologically. So many that I often wonder if the bookmakers do not specially employ staff to invent plausible-sounding but utterly specious systems to lure gullible astrologers into parting with their money. It is easy enough to pick a yak by means of astrology. The problem is, it needs to be the correct yak. For this, most of the published systems are quite worthless.'

'Really, Master? But I've read so many of them in astrological journals.'

'Many of which give every indication that they have never been tried out even once, but are the empty product of someone's bathtime reverie. Many others – and we know this because we see a chart printed to prove that success – have worked once. I can pick a winner by choosing the yak whose name reminds me of my granny: that does not prove this to be a worthwhile method. A lucky hit, as any gambler knows, is no more than a will-o'-the-wisp, leading the unwary into the mire.'

'We need a method that works every time.' With a stick in my one hand and the remains of the shiraz in my other, I hesitated over which to use after such a comment. I chose the shiraz and answered him in mellow tones: 'Where do I begin to answer that, boy? We do not *need* any method at all. We would quite like to have one. Nor can we expect a method that works every time. There is no such method, in any form of astrology, and the world is all the better for it. Can you imagine what would happen if astrologers had an infallible method?' He looked at me without replying, clearly thinking the shiraz had the better of me. Little did the lad know that, accustomed as I am to the intoxicating effect of the rarefied air at the heights on which Master Astrologers dwell, vulgar intoxicants have no effect on the clarity of my thought. 'Have you ever met any astrologers?' I continued. 'But more to the point, whether the perfect method be desirable or not, it is impossible. God is perfect. The Creation is not God. Comprende?'

'Yes, Master.'

'If the Creation is not God, it therefore cannot be perfect.'

'But, Master: a yak can be a perfect yak; a raven can be a perfect raven. These things are not exclusive.'

'Pay attention, boy. Perfection is something that admits of no qualification. Something either is perfect or is not perfect. It cannot be a bit perfect. Creation is as perfect as Creation can be. This does not mean it is perfect. Britney may be as yakkish as any yak can be, but this does not make her perfect. For example, no matter how yakkish, she will yet die. This is evidence of change, while that which is perfect cannot change.'

'So the thing can be a very good example of its own kind, but that doesn't mean it's perfect.'

'Exactly. It's a very good Creation. But it is not perfect. It cannot be. Look.' As I spoke, Sedna fluttered down from my shoulder to sit on Britney's back, just in front of the boy. With his beak he carved the logic into her hair:

$$God = Perfect$$
$$Creation \neq God$$
$$\therefore Creation \neq Perfect$$

'Oh!' he exclaimed, 'I see.'
'Were you taught this at astrology kindergarden?'
'No, Master.'
'That is a tragedy, because the whole of astrology derives from this one fact. Astrology takes place within the Creation. Perfection is not ours to have. There is always a slippage between the big plan and how things work out on Earth. There cannot be otherwise. So the idea that there can be any perfect system within astrology is an illusion. One born of our arrogance.' We stopped for a moment to admire the view, the empty mountains striving for the sky, and, below, the tiny moving specks of colour that were others making their slow way to the fair.

The boy was impatient to be on his way. I was not sure this attraction to the gaudy life of the village was testimony to a desire to be a Master Astrologer. But he was yet young. As I helped him up onto Britney's back again, he asked me, 'Tell me more of these systems for picking the winner, Master. Can we check birthcharts?'
'You have the birthchart of every jockey in the race?'
'No, Master.'
'Assuming you did, do you have an affection for long, hard labour?'
'No, Master.'
'For that is what would be required. Then remember, the jockey is not a sporting automaton, sprung to life only to ride: the success that we find in his chart does not necessarily take place on the track. Even if it does, he will be riding five or six races during the afternoon. No matter how closely we study his chart, we will not be able to determine which of these he will win. Or consider the measure of success: he might come third in one race, last in the others, and still think that a successful day, though we might disagree. We might find clues in his chart, but the amount of work needed to find them – opening the ephemeris and noticing that Jupiter is near his natal Sun is not enough! – is not repaid by the meagre prospects of success.'

'I meant the horses' birthcharts, Master.'

I was beginning to doubt the lad's sanity. 'How do you propose gathering timed charts for every horse in a race? It's hard enough to find reliable birth-data for humans. To complicate things further, all race-horses – at least in Britain – have the same official birthday. That makes gathering their true charts even more difficult. Then, while racing fans might assure us that, left to their own devices, horses would organize race-meetings for the sheer thrill of running, we might doubt whether coming first is really that important to the horse.' Britney grunted in agreement. 'Or the yak,' I added, patting her neck.

'The owners, the trainers?'

'Same problem, my boy. They too have a life outside the sport. An owner is likely to have many interests, both on and off the turf. A trainer is likely to have several horses running. And,' I leaned over so I could whisper, 'some idle fellows have suggested that running the horse to lose may sometimes be seen as a success.' He looked aghast.

I thought about offering him a swig of my shiraz to help him recover his composure, but with a long day ahead of us decided that was unwise. A smart tap from my stick worked just as well. 'OK,' he continued, 'Birthcharts are out. Can we use horary?'

'In principle, yes. But we are beset with limitations. Let's work through the possibilities. First, as I've told you before, we cannot use horary mechanically. The sheer frequency of races is the problem. Someone who is asking *Who will win the 2.30 at Kempton Park?* is likely also to be asking *Who will win the 3.00 at Kempton Park?* to say nothing of the 2.35 at Sandown, the 2.40 at Ascot and whatever else is happening in that day's programme. Day after day. Horary is not a coin-in-the-slot machine.'

'But what if our querent isn't an avid punter, and is asking only about the occasional race?'

'A horary may work if it is the annual question for the Grand National or the Melbourne Cup: *Who will win?* We are picking the winner from a field. So we would look for the first aspect made to or by the ruler of the 10th house. The planet aspected will, by association of name, give us the winning horse.'

'That sounds simple enough.'

I repressed a laugh and continued: 'Often, though, when we come to racing we have a problem in determining what is the real question. Where does the querent's real interest lie? If I own the horse, or a share in the horse, there is a straightforward question: *Will my horse win?* A 12th-house matter. Or so it would seem, for often the horse is scarcely important, so the real question becomes *Will I win?* Or, more often, *Will I make a profit?'*

'So it could be a 12th-house question, a 1st-house question, or a 2nd-house question.'

'Yes, you begin to see the problem. And I'm sure I could find a few more houses, if I put my mind to it. Now, suppose I don't own the horse. There are a few horses who attract their own fan-club, so occasionally the question might seem to be *Will we win?* with the horse taken as "us" in the same way that a favourite football team is "us". But scratch a little and you will usually find that the real question here is *Will I profit by backing Golden Socks?* so it is a profit question, not a contest question.'

'But suppose the querent isn't betting?'

'Then it is most unlikely that the querent will be asking this question. Perhaps it could be asked, apparently as a matter of curiosity; but why? If not for profit, then most likely as a supposed test of horary. So the real question is not *Will Golden Socks win?* but *Does horary work?* Anyone who asks that as a horary question is a fool.'

'Could it be a 7th-house question, though? Maybe someone asks if Golden Socks will win, without having any special interest in Golden Socks.'

'You're thinking too much, my boy. It's most unlikely that we will find a valid 7th-house question, a question about "any old horse", because it's most unlikely that such a question will be asked except by someone who hopes to make money from the prediction. So the question is not really the question as asked, *Will Golden Socks win?* but the question the querent has in mind, *Will I profit by backing Golden Socks?'*

'But surely the two will give the same answer?'

'It might seem so. Do you have a computer in your home-land?'

'Yes, Master.'

'Then you will be aware that the computer cannot read your mind. It does what you tell it to do, not what you mean to tell it to do. This can be most frustrating. It's much the same with horary. If there is a discrepancy between the question as asked and the question as really meant, we have a problem. The artist will be looking for one thing, while something else is shown in the chart. The artist will ignore that something else, because it isn't relevant to the question as asked. Yet if the question as asked really is the question, it's that something else that will not be relevant.'

'It's confusing, Master.'

'Because the question is so confused. Occasionally, it can be clear enough. If the owner asks *Will my horse win the 2.30?* we would take Lord 12 for the horse, the 10th house and Lord 10 to signify victory. Then we would judge in exactly the same way as we have done with *Will my team win the league?* [27] We must use the radical 10th house, not the turned 10th (the 10th house from the 12th): we are concerned with the horse winning the race, not with his career prospects.'

'That's clear enough, Master.'

'As we're discussing the horse's owner as querent, answer me this: suppose the question were *Should I buy this horse?* Which accidental dignity would we look for?'

He thought for a while. 'Cazimi?' he asked, without much conviction.

'The horse's significator cazimi would be most encouraging, yes. But that's not really something we could go looking for. It either is cazimi or it isn't, and that is obvious from the chart.'

'Conjunct Regulus?'

'That too would be encouraging. But that too isn't something we would need to check. It's either there or it isn't. Think: what does the owner want the horse to do?'

'To win races, Master.'

'And how will it do that?'

'By running, Master.'

'So....?' His expression showed that his brain had seized up. I gave him a tap on the head to free the machinery, but to no avail. 'Think about it. You'll find the answer in Appendix 3. In the meantime, here are some people you should meet.'

We had stopped outside a cave, from whose depths a squawk from Sedna brought two men hurrying to greet us. One was full of youthful vigour and had the most piercing eyes, that seemed as clear and sharp as those of an eagle; the other so old he could have been the twin of the mountain on which he stood, yet possessed of a nobility of bearing that gave his every word or motion the quality of a stone dropping into a silent pool.

'Show respect,' I whispered to the lad, 'for these are the best friends an astrologer could ever have.' I spoke louder now, extending my hands towards them, 'Let me introduce my learned friends, Dr Reason and Dr Experience.'

The boy looked surprised. 'Were not these same the good friends of whom Nicolas Culpeper wrote, so long ago?'

'The very same,' I beamed. 'Once they dwelt in the city's din, which is where Master Culpeper encountered them, but so little are they regarded today, so rarely

---

[27] Pages 55–60 above.

sought or consulted, that driven by sheer indifference they have forsaken the city for a hermit life among these mountains. No one, alas, has noticed they have gone.'

I could see the boy was pleased to meet them, though I knew he could as yet have no inkling of how important they could be to him, if only he would spend some moments making their acquaintance. To encourage this, I invited them to accompany us to the fair. Bored with their isolated life, for both craved the company which could share their insights, they gladly agreed to join us. Sedna forsook my shoulder for a spot on Dr Reason's. The two had a special fondness for each other and immediately began chatting in the language of the birds.

As we set off again, I continued: 'Henry Coley, Lilly's protege, gives two horary methods in his *Key to the Whole Art of Astrology*.[28] These he took from the Arab astrologer Haly. One is for questions of the type *Will Golden Socks win?* the other for the general *Who will win?* Both rely on the placement and condition of the Lord of the Hour.'

I wasn't sure if his brain had completely ungummed itself yet, so thought I had best explain. 'The times from sunrise to sunset and sunset to sunrise are each divided into twelve equal sections. These are the astrological hours. Unlike our clock hours, they vary in duration from day to day and from latitude to latitude. The Lord of the Hour is the planet that rules each hour. The day is regarded as starting at dawn. The hour beginning at dawn is ruled by the same planet that rules the day: the Moon for Monday, Mars for Tuesday, Mercury Wednesday, Jupiter Thursday, Venus Friday, Saturn Saturday and the Sun Sunday. The order of the hour rulers is that of the Chaldean order of the planets: Saturn, Jupiter, Mars, Sun, Venus, Mercury, Moon. So on Monday the first hour is ruled by the Moon, the second by Saturn, then Jupiter, then Mars, and so on. On a Tuesday, the first hour is ruled by Mars, then the Sun, Venus, Mercury, Moon, Saturn, and so on.'[29]

'That's simple enough, Master.'

'Yes. Coley's method for *Will Golden Socks win?* is to cast a horary chart and locate the Lord of the Hour. If it is in the 1st house, the horse will win. In the 3rd, 10th or 11th, it will come second. In the 7th, neither first nor last. In the 4th, last. If the Lord of the Hour or Lord 1 is in its fall, the jockey will be nervous and may fall off. If adversely aspected, he may be injured.'

---

[28] London, 1676; reprinted Nottingham, n.d., p. 231-2. Bonatti gives much the same methods, and may indeed have been Coley's true source: *Book of Astronomy*, pp. 618-620; trans. Dykes, Minnesota, 2007.

[29] If you want to know what an Hour looks like, see Rubens' *The Fall of Phaethon*. The women in this painting are Hours.

'And what about his method for the general *Who will win?*'

'This gets more complicated, and his exposition is confused. Again, we cast a horary and locate the Lord of the Hour. If it is in the 1st, 10th or 11th house, the winning horse will be of the same colour as any planet which is in one of those three houses.'

'What if there are lots of planets in those houses?'

'Quite. What he seems to mean is that we judge by the Lord of the Hour itself, wherever it is. If the Lord of the Hour is in one of those houses and has good essential dignity, the winner will be among the favourites. The winner's odds lengthen as the Lord of the Hour's dignity decreases. In any of the other houses, with dignity, the winner's odds will be a bit longer. In any other house with no dignity, it will be a rank outsider. If the Lord of the Hour is oriental, the horse will be young; occidental, it will be old. In the 4th, it will be very old.'

'I don't understand, Master. Why should we abandon all our usual horary principles for these particular enquiries? We don't judge any other questions solely from the Lord of the Hour.'

I gestured to him to address his questions to Dr Reason, who was, as always, pleased to answer. 'You are right to ask, boy. We cannot accept things only because they are written in books. Even if the books are very old! As my good friend, Nicky Culpeper, wrote:[30]

LET EVERYONE THAT DESIRES TO BE CALLED BY THE NAME OF ARTIST HAVE HIS WITS IN HIS HEAD (FOR THAT'S THE PLACE ORDAINED FOR THEM) AND NOT IN HIS BOOKS

At the most generous assessment, what we have here is the tattered remnants of what was once a workable system. As it stands, it is certainly not usable.' He turned to me, smiling, 'The lad shows promise. He raised exactly the right objection.'

'He has an aptitude,' I confessed.

The good Doctor continued. 'But that would be a generous assessment of the method. This sounds more like fairground astrology. An astrology of amusement. Fortune-telling. Something which enables the practitioner to give a quick answer to someone whom he will never see again, or who is not taking the prediction so seriously.'

'Like newspaper horoscope columns?' the lad chipped in.

---

[30] Nicholas Culpeper, *Astrological Judgment of Diseases from the Decumbiture of the Sick,* p. 67; London, 1655, reprinted Nottingham, n.d.

'Yes, boy, much the same.'

'So, Master, I shouldn't use Coley's method when we get to the village?'

'I think Dr Reason has adequately answered that, don't you?'

We went on in silence for a while, save for Sedna and Dr Reason squawking at each other. Dr Experience was content to gaze upon the view, keeping his opinions until they might be required. Britney seemed absorbed in her own thoughts, as was the lad. At a moment when the squawking pair had moved some distance in front of us, he pulled gently on my sleeve.

'Master,' he began, in a voice scarcely louder than silence, 'you remember when Dr Reason said I had raised exactly the right objections to Coley's method?'

'Yes, my boy.'

'Well, Master, he was pleased with me. But I didn't say that because I had reasoned it. Coley's methods just sort of...didn't sound right.'

I laughed aloud and clasped him to my bosom. 'You must make closer acquaintance with the good Doctor. As yet your knowledge of him is based on rumour and misapprehension more than truth. Reason is not only the cold logic of dusty texts. Properly ordered, it is as beautiful as a goddess, leaning down from the heavens to bestow a kiss upon our brow. You say Coley's words didn't sound right. That is reason too. The music – the music of reason – was discordant. You heard it. For me, I smell it. Coley's words don't smell right. Some feel it. Some see it.'

He seemed to follow me. I continued, 'Clarity is all that is required: some dim perception of that divine clarity, in whichever way it strikes us. No one is asking mental somersaults of you, my boy. Now, let's catch them up. We draw closer to the village, and must consider other methods before we arrive.'

I shouted to attract Dr Reason's attention, then asked him to comment on other methods of predicting winners. He turned to the lad with a question: 'What is it, boy, that wins a horse-race?'

His face assumed that expression of valiantly struggling through thick fog with which I was so familiar. 'This is not a complicated question, my boy. Tell me: what will win a horse-race?'

He gave up valiantly struggling, suggesting, 'A horse?'

'Yes! A horse. This is a simple fact. But most theories of predicting races by the stars ignore it. Many theories, usually deriving from Sepharial's "silver key", use the stars to pick a winning weight. But what is the weight? It has no direct connection to the horse that carries it. It is, indeed, an obstacle, designed to prevent the horse running faster. Why should we see this weight in the stars?'

'It makes no sense, Doctor.'

'That is, alas, rarely a barrier between astrological theory and the bookshelf. As dear Nicky once said – oh, how I miss him – "Many authors invented whimsies, and when they had done, set them down to posterity for truth".[31] Even if the calculation of weight is presented in such awe-inspiring manner as

$$d = \frac{(x-9)\,4n}{81} + 4$$

as it is by Mr Sutaria,[32] this idea is still nonsense.'

'What does that have to do with astrology, Doctor?'

'Precious little, my boy. Then there are the theories that use the planets to select the number the winning horse is carrying.'

'But surely race numbers are doled out willy-nilly. The horse has no meaningful connection with the number it is wearing.'

'Exactly. As a bit of fine-sounding mumbo-jumbo the connection of planets with numbers has few peers. It was particularly popular in Theosophical circles, where fine-sounding mumbo-jumbo was the order of the day. At its root, there is a profound and beautiful connection: if ever you want to submit your brain to some rigorous exercise, try reading – or better yet, understanding – Iamblichus' *Theology of Arithmetic*, which treats the subject in depth. But that true connection was long forgotten by the time the modern sages decided to shovel the newly discovered planets into the pattern. That would have been desecration, had there been anything sacred left for them to desecrate. But even if we allow the connection between number and planet, there is no essential connection between number and horse.'

'So it makes no sense to select the horse by number.'

'Quite. Then there are other theories that use colour.'

'But, Doctor, horses don't come in many colours.'

'No, they don't. So for want of green horses, the theoreticians switch their attention from horse to rider. They use the colour of the jockey's silks.'

Dr Experience, who had been listening in silence, interrupted: 'I have yet to see a jockey carrying the horse past the winning-post. When I do, I will admit that it is jockeys, not horses, who win races.'

Dr Reason's smile showed he had reached the same conclusion. He continued, 'So we have some dubious, though popular, ways of connecting planet to horse. We also have dubious, and equally popular, ways of selecting the planet that will show the winner. There is a trap into which so many theories fall:

[31] op. cit., p. 68.
[32] R.L. Sutaria, *Astrology of the Race Course*, p. 93; Bombay, n.d.

THERE ARE A LOT OF CHARTS OUT THERE – NOT JUST THE ONE YOU HAVE UNDER YOUR NOSE

Forgetting that produces so much unsound theorising.'

'True words! True words, indeed, Dr Reason,' I threw in. 'This forgetfulness is the reason for a high proportion of the garbage that masquerades as astrology in all its branches. That Venus-Neptune square means you're an alcoholic – you and the billion others with whom you share that square. Pluto transiting your Sun means you will die – you and everyone else who shares your birthday.' Sedna pecked at my ear, warning me I was beginning to rant. I heeded his advice and gave space to wiser tongues.

Dr Reason resumed his argument: 'We are making our way down to the village. The nearest neighbouring village is a day's journey from there. The nearest village that holds yak races is far, far away, and races both here and there are held only once a year, on different days. This is not the situation with which you will be dealing when you leave here, my boy.'

'No. Races elsewhere are everyday occurrences.'

'Consider England – a country so small I could hold it in the palm of my hand. Crammed into that small space there will be at least three race meetings on any afternoon. Seven, eight, or even more on a Saturday. Each of these meetings will have races starting at thirty-minute intervals. Even though these start times will be staggered from course to course, they will produce similar charts. If a planet is near the Midheaven when the 2.40 starts at Wincanton, it will be near the Midheaven at the 2.30 at Uttoxeter and the 2.45 at Lingfield. If we are choosing the most angular planet as our winner – a common theory – we will find the planets take it in turns to dominate three or four races. Often more. So we would expect the winners in those races to have similar weights, numbers, colours, or names. This does not happen.'

Dr Experience added: 'If, for instance, the horse carrying the heaviest handicap winning at Uttoxeter were usually followed by the horse carrying the heaviest handicap winning at very other race within the next ten or fifteen minutes, we might expect Joe Punter to have noticed this. Similarly if victory for the jockey wearing red usually began a fashion for victories for jockeys wearing red.'

'Right, as ever, my friend,' continued Dr Reason. 'No matter what criterion we use for linking planet to horse, we must have a more subtle method for distinguishing the correct planet. It is easy to present an isolated example showing that the planet nearest the Ascendant or nearest the MC gives the winner. It is easy to find isolated examples demonstrating whatever hare-brained theory you might concoct. That is not proof that the method works.'

'Tell him about planetary hours,' I suggested.

'Sutaria suggests we use the Lord of the Hour to give us the planet.[33] He refines this by introducing a sub-ruler for each 5-minute segment of the hour. Even so, the sub-ruler is just that: a sub-ruler. It will qualify, but not overrule, the hour-ruler. So we still have the same problem: what wins at Uttoxeter should win at Wincanton ten minutes later. It doesn't.'

I could see that the boy's eagerness was turning to agitation. I could guess why. Once Dr Reason starts, it is hard to make him stop, and our destination was at hand. I addressed the learned pair: 'Well have you shown that these theories are built on sand. But have you tested them? Just in case.' Dr Experience spoke not, but in a gesture more eloquent than any words turned out his pockets, revealing them as containing nothing but dust.

By now the lad was tugging at my sleeve. 'Master, we're nearly at the village now. I've been told a lot of what not to do. What am I to do?'

'You think that was worthless converse, boy? Breath spent for nothing? Are you thinking of making a wager on these yak races?'

'Yes, Master,' he beamed, producing a shiny coin from his pocket.

'You see, we have saved you some money.' I took the coin he was holding as payment. I needed a new stick. 'Now, if you want something that works, try this:

John Addey's system

'Addey, one of the foremost among British astrologers of the twentieth century, published this method in *The Astrological Journal*, saying that in it "I place my trust after trying it on well over a thousand races"[34] – a degree of trial that contrasts with the "one lucky hit" system so favoured by writers on this subject.'

'I too have tested it thoroughly,' added Dr Experience. 'I tried it on every race in Britain and many abroad over a period of around three years. That's a lot of races.'

The boy's eyes were brighter than the desert sun at noon. 'And it works every time?'

---

[33] op. cit., p. 84. Sutaria's treatment of planetary hours is most original.

[34] Vol 2, No 2 (1960) pp. 16-18. Charles Carter makes a glancing reference to a similar system in a footnote to his *Essays on the Foundations of Astrology*, London, 1947(?), p. 156. My thanks to Christian Borup for pointing this out to me.

The good doctor laughed. 'No, my boy. Certainly not. But it is not necessary for a system to provide infallibility, or anything approaching infallibility, for it to be valid. All it need do is provide a better result than not using the system. This, Addey's method certainly does. It gives a significant edge over time.'

'So I can't guarantee that it will give me the winners at this afternoon's yak races?'

The doctor looked at me with disappointment. 'I thought you had been teaching the lad,' he said. 'So why does he still have these ideas about guarantees and infallibility?'

I shrugged. 'He's incorrigible. But he's young.'

'Yes,' the doctor agreed. 'Time will teach him what you have not.' I helped Time in its mission by whacking the lad on the back of the head. That jolted these ideas from him for a while, returning him to a more realistic frame of mind.

'Tell me then, Master, how this system works.'

'Set the chart for the time and place of the race, using Campanus cusps.'

'Why Campanus?' he asked, startled.

'I have no idea. I can see no reason for using it for anything else – though Addey regarded its efficacy here as validating Campanus for other uses.[35] It works, so let's use it.'

'OK, so we have the chart. Then what?'

'Regard everything else in the chart as standing still. Move the 5th cusp through its sign till it makes an aspect with a planet. The first planet it aspects shows the winning horse.'

'Yes, Master. But how?'

RACING CHECKLIST

Set chart for time and place of the race.
Campanus houses.
Keep planets still.
Move 5th cusp forward (anticlockwise) to first aspect.

Choose horse by: name association
                       house rulership
                       other accidental points
                       association by horse's nature.

---

[35] ibid.

'Primarily by the symbolism of name. If the planet is Mars and *Soldier Boy* is running, that's our horse. If the planet is Mercury and there's a horse called *Pickpocket*. If the planet is Saturn and there's a *Mr Grumpy* or *Black Jewel*. Blessed are those horses with nice names, like *Uranus Collonges*; forever accursed those whose names seem a meaningless jumble of letters.'

'Master!' He was blushing. You've mentioned...' he dropped his voice so the good doctors couldn't hear, 'Uranus.'

'Oh, yes. We're off to the races, boy. We can afford to let our hair down. You can throw in Uranus, Neptune and Pluto. Chiron, if you like. Asteroids. Addey used all sorts. Minor aspects, too. Addey found they worked "including certainly the quintile group down to 18°".[36] Dr Experience told me they do work down to that level, but not beyond it.'

'Picking by name is all very well, Master, but what if Mars is our planet and *Soldier Boy* is running – but so are *Red Devil* and *Invasion Force*?'

'That's a good question. Be aware of other factors. For example, if that Mars were retrograde and the famous *Red Rum* were one of our Mars candidates, we could choose that because it is "murder" backwards. The accuracy of definition in these charts can be breath-taking. I had a chart once where the winner was shown by the Moon in Leo in the term of Mercury: *Sunday News and Echo*.'

'That's wonderful, Master! Sun-day for Leo; news for Mercury; echo for the Moon.'

'We can also use our common sense and narrow down the options by the horses' odds. That 50/1 shot might look tempting to the astrologer, but if it's going off at 50/1 it probably can't run any faster than you can.'

'Are there other connections besides the planet's natural rulerships?'

'Certainly. Look at the house or houses the planet rules in the chart for the race. These may either complement the planet's natural rulerships, helping us pick one of several possibilities, or replace them altogether.'

'Sounds complicated.'

'Not really. Remember that when you are doing this, you have the race-card in front of you. You are not trying to pull the winning name out of the air. You have only a limited number of names, one of which should fit. With house rulerships, Lord 12 might show *Dungeon Master*; Lord 5 *Party Girl*. Look too at what else is happening to the planet. A planet combust gave *Surfeit of Sun* as a winner. Opposed by Saturn might give *Against the Clock*; slow in motion could give *Slowcoach*.'

'What about those horses whose names are incomprehensible?'

[36] ibid.

'Ha! Yes, a knowledge of Arabic would be a useful asset. A knowledge of Klingon, too. Sometimes we can only admit defeat. But there can be ways past this obstacle. The Sun can show the favourite, regardless of its name. Then, the racing papers will give brief descriptions of the horses. Obviously enough, an unusually old horse, or the only black in a field, would be shown by Saturn. A very big horse by Jupiter. But Uranus gave a winner described as "somewhat eccentric" and – my favourite of all – Mercury pointed to *Mutashim*, a horse whose name baffled me, but who was, the press said, "a bit of a thinker". The general rule seems to be: if there is a straight planet-horse connection, take that; if not, hunt around for another possibility.'

'But what if I can't find any connection at all?'

'First, look again. You may well have missed something. But if you really can't find any connection between the first planet aspected and a horse, try the next planet aspected by the 5th cusp. It's almost as if the first planet would have shown the winner, if only a horse of that nature had been running. But it isn't, so we may pass on to the next choice.'

'We do seem to be working with an awful lot of choices, Master, if we are using all those pieces of astral debris and even trivial aspects.'

'Yes. I would counsel restraint with the number of celestial bodies you involve. When you go back to your homeland, you will no doubt be using a computer with, no doubt, young and eager as you are, some fancy software that will fill the screen with asteroids and the like. You will observe that in this mountain fastness we have no such equipment. Sedna has memorised the ephemerides of a small number of the more useful asteroids, but the great majority of them will only get in your way. Maybe you'll miss the odd winner if you don't use them; you will certainly miss many winners if you do, through grabbing at asteroids when a real planet is crying out for your attention.'

'Are they useful at all, then, Master?'

'I've seen Vesta, goddess of the hearth, show *Hobbs* as a winner. And Lancelot showing, for example, *Sir Tasker*. Lancelot is the most useful of them, as there are so many horses with knightly names. If you plan to make a long study of this method, try throwing them in and see how they work. Personally, I favour speed and simplicity over exhaustive detail. If I were doing this now I'd keep to the main planets. After all, how much effort do you want to expend on these charts?'

'And all those aspects, too!'

'There is a hierachy, both with planets and aspects. As a general rule in these charts:

* the more minor the aspect the less likely it is to work
* the more minor the 'planet' the less likely it is to work.

So if the 5th cusp makes a minor aspect first, then a trine immediately after that, you'd do well to go for the trine. Or if it aspects Ceres first, then Mars a degree or two after that, go for Mars. Unless one of the horses running is called *Harvest Festival*! If the minor aspect or asteroid links clearly with one of the horses, go with that.'

'So what you're saying, Master, is that I should use my discretion, depending on the names of the horses running.'

'Exactly. Always remember: the astrologer is an artist, not a mechanic.'

'Yes, Master. We're nearly at the village now; the races will soon be starting. Can we look at some charts?'

'Certainly. These charts are so simple that there is little point in working through numerous examples, or in me giving you test charts to judge on your own. Here are a few to give you the idea.' I drew the charts on Britney's coat as we walked.

'This is the one John Addey used in his article. It is for the Grand National in 1960, run some weeks after the article was printed (right, top).

The 5th cusp applies to a minor aspect – 105° – with the Sun. The race went to the favourite, *Merryman II*, at 13/2. Here's another (right, bottom). Which planet shows our winner?'

'The 5th cusp makes a square to Mercury. So a Mercury horse.'

'Yes. Mercury rules the 2nd house. The winner was *Grand Lucre* at 11/2. Now look at this one (page 146, top), which shows how precise these charts are. See how similar this chart is to the last one?'

'They're virtually identical, Master. Mercury wins again.'

'Look again. I know we left those little creatures in the cave, but that is no excuse for forgetting them.'

'Ah, Mars! The cusp makes an immediate conjunction with Mars, by antiscion.'

'Yes. The winner was *Strike Force*, at 2/1.'

'So why didn't Mars win in the previous chart?'

'Take a look. Work out where its antiscion falls. You see: it's already separated from the cusp. Here's another chart, again very similar (page 146, bottom).'

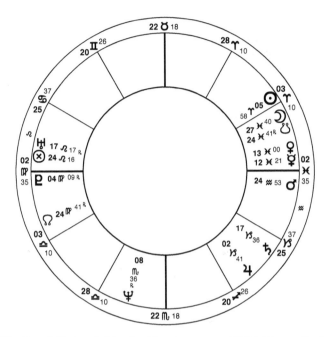

The Grand National, March 26th 1960, 3.15 pm GMT, Aintree, England.

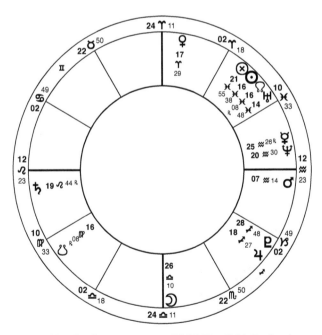

March 7th 2007, 2.30 pm GMT, Lingfield, England.

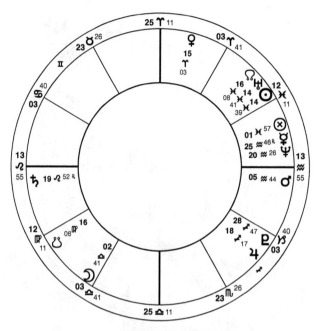

March 5th 2007, 2.50 pm GMT, Wolverhampton, England.

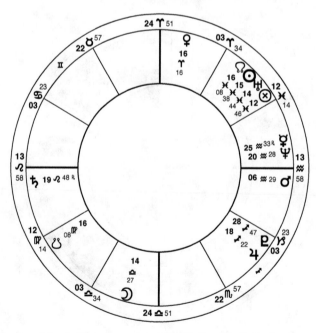

March 6th 2007, 2.40 pm GMT, Southwell, England.

'It's Mars again, Master. Conjunction by antiscion.'

'Yes. Mars rules the 10th. *Government* won at 66/1. There's just time for one last one, before you must start calculating your own for this afternoon's races.'

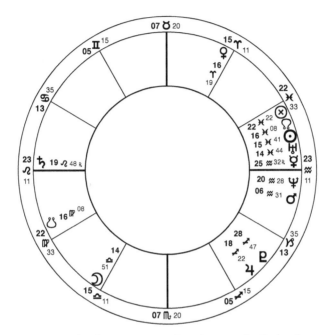

March 6th 2007, 3.30 pm GMT, Newcastle, England.

'The cusp makes a semi-square to Neptune.'

'Yes. Or we may prefer a proper aspect to a proper planet and take the sextile to Mars, which is Lord 9. Either way, we get the winner: *In Dreams*, at 4/1.'

And so we reached the village, where the lad spent an enjoyable – and profitable – afternoon forecasting the yak races, while the good doctors, Sedna and myself relaxed in the kvass tent and Britney renewed old acquaintance and struck up new. As evening fell, we made our farewells and set off back along that long, winding path.

Once I had relieved the boy of his winnings, to defray necessary expenses, he had some questions: 'Why is it, Master, that the connection by name is valid, while you say that the connection by weight or number is not?'

'Name is something far more significant than is often recognised today. It seems to modern man that a name is a label stuck on more or less arbitrarily, which can

just as arbitrarily be changed. The tradition, however, stresses its extreme importance, for name belongs to the essence of the thing named. It is the recognition of
that essence, in much the same way that Adam saw all the animals, understood
them in their essence and thus named them.[37] We see this, for instance, at
baptism, where we are given a Christian name, that name by which God knows us.
Our full name is then a combination of our essence-name (Luke or John) and our
accident-name, as shown by our social function (Baker, Butcher) or some other
reference to our material nature (Brown, Long, son of).'

'So the horse's name relates to the horse at a much profounder level than the
accidents of the weight it must carry or the number it is given for that race. That
makes sense.'

'It is, my boy, in this connection of planet and name that we find the true use-
fulness of this system. As you saw, even if you win, the profits don't last long. But
the study of the planet-name connection brings a lasting profit.'

'Oh, Master. How can I get that profit which lasts?'

'Astrology is like a language. To use it well, we must learn to speak it like a
native. Regardless of which horse wins the race, this system offers an excellent
training in astrological fluency. I want to see you practicing this.'

'But how?'

'When you're learning a language you can increase your fluency by putting
things you see into that language. We can do the same with astrology. We see the
fire in the mouth of our cave: Mars conjunct Saturn. Or Mars in the 4th house.
But if we do this, we tend to pick and choose: we go for the easy puzzles. Working
our way through a race-card, translating the horses' names into astrology, makes
it harder to duck the difficult ones.'

'So I can do that without even setting a chart?'

'Yes. Then, as a different exercise, set the chart for that race and see how many
horses you can connect with the planets. It's most valuable.'

'I'll do that, Master. But I have another question. Doesn't this system run into
that same difficulty of "there's a lot of charts out there"?'

'No. Because the method of choosing the planet is much more precise. Taking
aspects from a moving cusp can select different planets in charts that are almost
identical. The great virtue of this system is its time-sensitivity. But this is also its
greatest drawback.'

'How so, Master?'

'Around a quarter of races go off sufficiently late that judgement from these

---

[37] Genesis 2:19-20.

charts is redundant. But the system works sufficiently well on the others to give an edge over the odds if it is used consistently.'

'What about these minor aspects and asteroids. If they work here, shouldn't I be using them in other charts?'

I had been waiting for this one. I weighed my stick in my hand, judging the best angle of approach. But then desisted. It had been a long day. The fumes from the festivities had no doubt affected his brain, with what I hoped would be a temporary affliction. 'You will note that even in these charts those strangers to sound astrology are used but little. We are scraping the bottom of the astrological barrel here. Unless we are to cast charts to see which raindrop will hit the ground first, there is little we can do that is more trivial than determining which horse will win one of many races on any given afternoon. Those bits of cosmic flotsam are up there; there are minor resonances around the chart, as there will be in any field: if these petty points have some scope to come out and play here, that does not mean they have significance in charts cast for anything even slightly less trivial.'

We had arrived at the doctors' cave. As we shook hands in parting, Dr Experience reached into his store to share something with the lad: 'There is a mystery here, which is the frequency with which this system identifies steamers.'

He glanced at me, too shy to ask the doctor what he meant. 'Horses that attract a great deal of betting interest, and so fall rapidly in price,' I whispered.

'I often found,' the doctor continued, 'this method gave a horse who closed from outsider to favourite, or near it, and then did nothing in the race. It is possible that the nation's betting-shops are filled with astrologers using this system, so all backing the same nag. But it is unlikely. I wonder, then, whether this system is identifying something other than the winner – I don't know quite what – and this something happens to coincide with the winner on a significant number of occasions. The answer to this may lie in the use of the 5th house, which isn't something we would use for any other sporting purpose.'

'You have given us something to think about there, my dear Doctor,' I told him as I clasped his hand. I could see he was sorry to take his leave of the lad; Dr Reason too. The boy himself had tears hanging inside his eyes, from where they twinkled like stars as they caught the moonlight. I said nothing, but knew their parting would not be long. His time with me was drawing to a close. One more subject to cover, then he would leave, for I had no more to teach him. Then he would come back here, taking Dr Reason and Dr Experience with him as tutors and boon companions when he returned to the world. What better company could he have?

INTERLUDE:

THE GREATEST RACEHORSE EVER?

A horse going off at odds of 1/70? A horse undefeated throughout his career of 18 races, winning 8 of them as walkovers? That might seem a successful horse, but in his progeny this horse was more successful yet. As his biographer, Nicholas Clee, writes:

Ninety five per cent of thoroughbreds trace their descent to (him) in the male line and many of the remaining five per cent have him in their pedigrees. Every horse that ran in the 2006 Derby was a male line descendant...so was every horse that ran in the French Derby; and every horse that ran in the Kentucky Derby.[38]

Not only flat racers, but jumping legends such as Desert Orchid and Arkle trace their line to him. Impressive. But better still, his breeder, the Duke of Cumberland – 'the Butcher of Culloden' – had the decency to give him a proper astrological name. Oh, that more breeders would follow suit. Legend tells that he was born exactly on a solar eclipse, so he was named Eclipse.

Castor was one of the Dioscuri, famed as 'tamers of horses', so it is entirely fitting that the bright star Castor should be on the Ascendant here. This beast tamed every horse he encountered. Every birthchart shows both the nature of the person – or horse – born and the life through which that person moves. When looking at the life rather than the personality, the person – or horse – is shown by the Ascendant ruler, which in this chart is the Moon. He was born during a solar eclipse: the Moon overcomes and conceals the Sun's light. This is a powerful testimony of dominance. The eclipsed Sun is in Aries, where it is exalted: this horse is dominating even the very best.

His children and further descendants are shown by the 5th house and its ruler, Venus. In its own sign, Venus is strongly dignified: good progeny. Strongly dignified in a fixed sign: lastingly good progeny.

There is a puzzle here, however. The sign of a good racehorse is that it runs fast.

[38] *The Observer Sports Monthly*, March 2007, pp. 44-51.

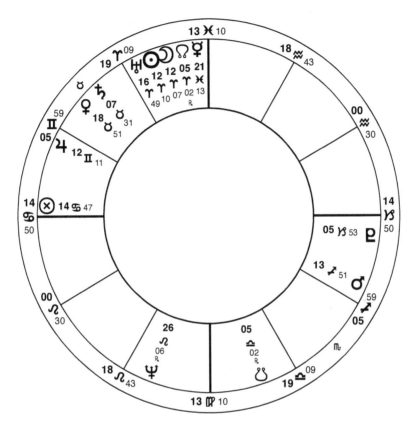

'Eclipse', April 1st 1764, 10.17 am LMT, Windsor, England.

But there is no speed here. The Moon, signifying Eclipse himself, is moving slowly. Nothing in the chart has any notable speed. How come he ran so fast? Fast enough to allow his owner to clean up on his famous bet of 'Eclipse first; the rest nowhere': every other horse beaten by a distance, so far behind that not one of them qualified for the next heat.

The answer to this puzzle is in the lasting dominance of this horse. Napoleon may have ruled a vast empire, but ninety-five per cent of all rulers today do not trace their blood-line to him! If the native is to stand out above the crowds in some way, we would usually look back to the previous eclipse to see where the power to do this is coming from. Having your own birthchart effectively plugged in to the chart for that eclipse is like being hot-wired into the mains: major power.

But Eclipse was born on an eclipse, so there is no eclipse chart to which we can hook up the power cables. We must take a step further up the astrological scale, looking at the chart for the previous Great Conjunction. These conjunctions of Jupiter and Saturn happen only every twenty years, so have far more power to offer than eclipses, which are, comparatively speaking, two a penny.

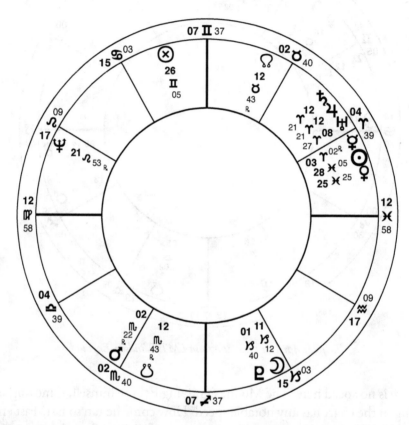

Great Conjunction, March 18th 1762, 4.41 pm GMT, Windsor, England.

The Jupiter/Saturn conjunction was at 12 Aries. Eclipse's eclipse fell right on this point. Connections do not come any stronger: if being plugged in to an eclipse chart is like being wired into the mains, this is like being wired direct into a nuclear reactor. Power aplenty! Power, yes, but speed? The eclipse and conjunction are in Aries, a cardinal fire sign, which is fast moving. But that alone is nothing so exceptional, and Eclipse's speed certainly was exceptional.

At the time of their conjunction, both Jupiter and Saturn had their foot pressed hard down to the floor. Jupiter was covering over 14 minutes of arc per day; Saturn over 7. Both were moving at a speed they rarely attain. By hitting this conjunction, Eclipse's birthchart plugged him directly into the combination of power and speed that enabled him to leave his rivals standing over distances far exceeding those commonly raced today.

4

The question of profit

Next morning, our frugal breakfast of mountain water garnished with the scent of cooking rising from the village below was scarcely finished before he could contain himself no longer: 'Suppose, Master, the client does not ask about who will win or lose, but only about making a profit. How do we approach that?'

'With horary, my boy, the most efficient tool for most things astrological. It's an 8th-house question.'

'But isn't gambling a 5th-house matter, Master?'

I pointed towards the battered volume that he had drawn from his saddle-bag when first he arrived. He passed it to me. 'I thought you said you had studied *The Horary Textbook*,' I said, as I smacked him on the head with it, wondering if that were the only way the information it contained could ever be infused to his brain. 'Let's be serious about this. If someone is gambling, what do they want?'

'To win.'

'Yes. But we can win without staking money. Is it the mere satisfaction of being right that is desired?'

'No, Master. They want money.'

'And does the 5th house have anything to do with money?'

'Only if it is my father's money, 2nd house from the 4th.'

'Which isn't relevant here. A gambling question is a matter of profit. If you are betting, you are pitting your wits against someone else. That person is your enemy: 7th house. You want his money: 2nd house from the 7th, which is the 8th.' He looked unconvinced, so I continued. 'In essence, if you are placing a bet you are saying that your opponent is wrong. Maybe it is a friend who has called Heads and you think it will be Tails. Or maybe it is a bookmaker who has priced something at 4/1 when you think the true price should be only 2/1.'

'The Heads or Tails is clear enough. I don't follow the 4/1 and 2/1.'

'You think *Golden Socks* has a better chance of winning than is shown in the bookie's price. He may well not win, but if your judgement is consistently better than the bookie's you will, over time, show a profit.'

'So the bookie is my enemy and I want his money. But what if I'm playing poker with my friends? They are the 11th house and their money is 2nd from the 11th.'

This deserved a whack. 'No! You may be chummy enough with them, but within the context they are your enemies. Friends don't take each other's money.' When he had finished rubbing his head, I asked him, 'What, then, do we want to see in the chart?'

'AN APPLYING ASPECT BETWEEN LORD 8 AND LORD 1, THE MOON OR LORD 2.'

That whack had evidently done him good, so I gave him another as reward. 'Yes. We need an aspect connecting the querent – Lord 1 or the Moon – with the enemy's money, Lord 8. Or an aspect connecting Lord 8 with the querent's bank balance, Lord 2. Either of these will do just as well.'

'Does it matter which planet applies to which, Master? Whether the querent's planet goes to Lord 8 or Lord 8 goes to the querent's planet?'

'Not at all. This is a general rule in horary:

A'S PLANET GOING TO B'S PLANET DOESN'T MEAN A GOES TO B.

It can equally well show B going to A. This is true whether it is Granny coming to tea or the bookie's money coming to my pocket. It is the context that shows who is going to whom. The question assumes that a bet is made: my money goes to the bookie. There remain two alternatives: either my money stays with him or his money comes to me. If there is an aspect, his money comes to me. The default option – the "what happens if there is no testimony?" – is that my money stays with him.'

'So if I am signified by Venus and his money by Saturn, and Venus applies to Saturn, I win.'

'Yes.'

'And if I am signified by Saturn and his money by Venus, and Venus applies to Saturn, I win.'

'Yes.'

'And the Moon going to Lord 8 shows a win for me, too.'

'Yes: the Moon will be cosignificator of the querent unless it signifies either the bookie or his money. Unless, that is, Cancer is on either the 7th or the 8th cusp. In that case, the Moon will signify the bookie (7th cusp) or his money (8th cusp).'

'The aspect between my planet and Lord 8 must be applying?'

'Yes. Separating aspects have already happened, so they show things that have already happened. That is no use to us here: we want to know only what *will* happen. So we must have an applying aspect. Watch out, though, for translations and collections of light. They can give us a win.'

'And for prohibitions, Master!'[39]

'Yes, my boy.' He was trying so hard to please that I gave him a gentle tap on the head in approval.

'Does it matter what kind of aspect we have?'

'Indeed!

THE NATURE OF THE ASPECT IS IMPORTANT
Conjunctions, sextiles and trines are fine.
Squares show the event with delay or difficulty.
Opposition shows success, but it isn't worth the candle.

Within the context, squares aren't usually much of a problem. If you're betting with an individual you might have to harass him a bit before you get paid. Maybe if you're a high-roller, a square could show the bookie delaying the pay-out, or questioning the bet. Usually, though, the context doesn't allow of much in the way of problems.

'An opposition, though, is far more serious. Oppositions bring the event, but show it falling apart afterwards (Yes, you'll marry him, but it won't last) or coming together with regret (Yes, you'll marry him, but you'll wish you hadn't) or coming together but with so much effort that it just isn't worth it. That last of these is the most likely interpretation in these questions: OK, you'll win, but whatever the prize it doesn't justify the effort.'

'I remember that paragraph from *The Horary Textbook*.[40]

I once asked a horary about a bet on a football match. The chart showed Lord 2 applying to Lord 1 by opposition. This made no sense. How could my money come to me? Either my money would disappear or the bookie's money would come to me. Consumed

---

[39] See *The Horary Textbook*, chapter 9 for explanation of these terms.
[40] p. 160.

with curiosity, I placed the bet. The match was abandoned at half-time and all bets refunded. My money did come to me – by opposition, as I had the nuisance of having to make the journey to collect it.'

'Quite. We must also

CONSIDER THE ESSENTIAL AND ACCIDENTAL DIGNITY OF LORD 8

Think about these testimonies. What do they tell us about the success of the bet? You'll find the answers in Appendix 3.

1. Lord 1 applies to Lord 8 by square.
2. Lord 8 applies to Lord 1 by trine.
3. Lord 8 is cazimi and applies to Lord 1 by square.
4. Lord 2 applies by trine to Lord 8, which is in its fall.
5. The Moon goes to sextile Lord 8, which is on the North Node.
6. Lord 1 applies to oppose Lord 8, which is in its exaltation.

As you see, this consideration gives us information about the level of success we might expect.'

'Whether we win big or win small.'

'Exactly. In some contexts this information makes little or no difference: we win or we lose, with no scope for fine-tuning. But it can be most useful. The big or small is with reference to the size of the stake. Consider, for example, rugby matches. These are usually won by the favourites, so the bookies offer two prices: one price for the underdogs to win at very long odds, and a handicap price at much shorter odds. In the handicap, the underdogs are given an imaginary start of X points.'

'So the underdogs can lose the match, but the gambler who backs them will still win his bet if they lose by fewer than X points.'

'Exactly. So if you were thinking of backing the underdogs and the chart showed you would win a lot, you'd back them to win outright at long odds. If the chart showed that you will win, but not so much, you would go for the handicap price at shorter odds. Take a look at this chart. The question was: *Will I win by backing Hedgehunter in the Grand National?* What do you see?'

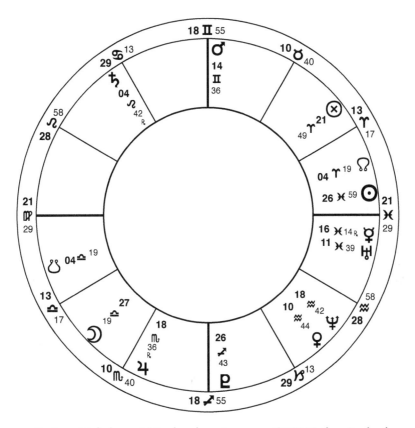

Profit on Hedgehunter? March 17th 2006, 5.42 pm GMT, Nailsea, England.

'First I find my significators.

Lord 1 is Mercury.

Lord 2 is Venus.

Cancer is not on the 7th or 8th cusps, so the querent also has the Moon.

Lord 8 is Mars.

Then I look for an aspect.

Hey, Venus goes to trine Mars!'

'And? What about Mercury?'

'Mercury is retrograde. So it goes back to square Mars.' He saw my fingers closing around my stick, so he hurriedly added, 'Though I'd have to check my ephemeris to make sure that aspect perfects.' My fingers relaxed. 'So we have two aspects. Does that mean we win twice?' My fingers unrelaxed. But this time a ferocious glare was enough.

'The void of course Moon, Master. What about that?'

'It's of no matter. A void Moon can always be overruled by other strong testimony, and here we have such testimony in abundance.'

'So the querent wins.'

'Yes. But look at Lord 8. What does this tell us about the bet? How should we advise the querent?'

'Mars is close to the MC, so it's accidentally quite strong. But essentially it has dignity only by face. That's next to nothing. There won't be a big win.'

'So what do we tell the querent?'

'Don't back a horse at long odds.'

This time I had to use my stick, even breaking it in the process. Sedna hopped into the cave to fetch me another. 'No, boy! We know which horse he is planning to back. That is given us in the question. What we're told here is that he will win, but the pay-out won't be great. So...?'

'Ah! We tell him not to punt on the nose, but to back the horse each-way.'

'Which would have been sound advice: *Hedgehunter* placed.'

Having given him some time to reflect on this, I posed him some questions about combustion. You'll find the answers in Appendix 3.

1. 'Suppose I have made a bet with my business partner on the outcome of a football match between our favourite teams. I cast a chart to see if I will win the bet. The ruler of the 8th house is combust. Am I happy or sad? Why?

2. And if the ruler of the seventh house were combust? Why?'

He had his 'I'm wondering about something, please ask me what it is' expression on. So I obliged. 'In that Hedgehunter chart,' he began, 'couldn't we have judged it as *Will this horse win?*'

I played him along. 'Suppose we had. What would be the first thing that would leap to your attention?'

'I'd have to start by looking at the 12th, the house of animals larger than goats.'

'What's special about the degree on its cusp? What is there?'

'Nothing in this chart, Master.' He was at a loss.

'28, 29 degrees of Leo. Finding a relevant planet or relevant cusp there should set an alarm bell ringing. Why? Because whatever is there is on Regulus, one of the brightest of stars and one of the few that can make a major contribution to horary judgement. It is *Cor Leonis*, the Heart of the Lion, a powerful testimony of success.'

'But he didn't win.'

'No. Regulus gives us an encouraging start, but it is by no means the whole of judgement. Is there an applying aspect between Lord 12, significator of the horse, and Lord 10, significator of victory?'

'The Sun and Mercury. No, they are heading in opposite directions.'

'Is Lord 12 immediately applying to conjunct the 10th cusp?'

'No.'

'Even if it were, we would like some supporting testimony for that. A planet's placement on a cusp can show no more than what is on the querent's mind – in this case, the thought of the horse winning. With support, though, such as Regulus provides here, it can become testimony of the event. Now, what about the Moon?'

'But you said the void of course Moon doesn't matter here.' In despair, I handed the stick Sedna had brought from the cave back to him, telling him to fetch one sturdier and to be quick about it. 'Pay attention, boy! I said it didn't matter in our previous judgement, because the void Moon can always be overruled by other strong testimonies. There, we had two such testimonies. Here, we have none.'

Desperate to redeem himself, he raced into the cave, returning before Sedna had time to select a suitable instrument of correction, bearing a small, furry thing in his arms. 'By antiscion, the Sun is on the South Node. That's a big negative.'

He had pleased me, so I waved Sedna away. 'Well said, my boy. If we were judging the question *Will this horse win?* that would be an important testimony. But there is one testimony more important yet – and that is that this was not the question asked. I've looked at this with you because it shows some points worth discussing. But I've looked at it with you purely as an exercise. We must be quite clear on this:

ANSWER ONLY THE QUESTION ASKED

Do resist the temptation to try reading the chart from every possible angle in the hope that you'll stumble upon an answer that you like. What we have done here is a judgement on a hypothetical question. If it did show victory for our horse, this would be in a hypothetical race – and would be followed only by hypothetical bookmakers paying out hypothetical money. That would be unlikely to satisfy our non-hypothetical querent.'

'Suppose it were my own horse, Master. Suppose I was wondering if I would win prize-money by running him.' Britney snorted. 'Or my own yak,' he added, moving smartly out of range of her back legs.

'In most cases such a question would be phrased as *Will my horse win?* and we've dealt with that before. But it is possible there might be a question about profit from the horse. That would be shown by the horse's 2nd house – the horse's money, as it were.'

'The 2nd from the 12th. But that's the 1st. How do we deal with that?'

'It depends on the question. Is it a specific question about money from one race, or is it a general question about profit from buying this horse? If it is a specific question, we would judge it in the same way as we have been discussing. We'd want an aspect between Lord 1, which in this case signifies the profit, because the 1st house is 2nd from the 12th...'

'So Lord 1 isn't the querent?' he interrupted.

'No. We have a clash of duties: Lord 1 could be either the querent or the thing asked about. Always in such cases we give the disputed planet to whichever is the main focus of the question.'

'So in this case, Lord 1 signifies the profit, because the profit is the focus of the question.'

'Exactly, my boy. Good. Unless Cancer is rising, this leaves us with the Moon to signify the querent. So an aspect between Lord 1 and the Moon would give a Yes. Or we could connect the profit with the querent's bank balance, as shown by Lord 2.'

'So money coming from the horse would be shown by an applying aspect between Lord 1 and either the Moon or Lord 2. What about Lord 12, the horse?'

'Irrelevant. We are discussing money, not horses. That said, though, finding dignified Jupiter, dignified Venus, or the North Node in the 12th would be a general indication of good things coming through the horse. But that wouldn't be conclusive testimony.'

'And if there is an aspect, we can assess the amount of the profit by the condition of Lord 1, just as we did with Lord 8 a moment ago.'

'Yes. Now, what will we look for in general profit questions, such as *Will I make money by buying Golden Socks?*'

He looked strangely inspired. I took a firm grip on my stick, as a precaution. Perhaps he was coming down with mountain-fever, brought on by the rarefied air at this height, which can induce acts of unseemly over-enthusiasm in would-be astrologers. 'That must be like a *profit from my knowledge* question!' he exclaimed, looking pleased with himself.[41]

I was pleased with him too, and showed this by relaxing my grip on the stick. 'Well done, my boy. Again, the profit is the horse's 2nd house, which is the radical 1st. Only this time we don't need an aspect. We can judge solely from the condition of Lord 1 and of the 1st house itself.'

---

[41] See *The Horary Textbook*, pp. 216-8.

'Suppose there is an aspect in the chart, maybe between Lords 1 and 2?'

'If there is one, we would have to take its nature into account. With a trine, sextile or conjunction, whatever profit there is comes easily. With a square, there will be delays or difficulties. That might show, for instance, a couple of barren seasons before the horse gets among the prizes. With an opposition, whatever profit there is won't be worth the lay-out. Maybe he wins you thousands, but costs you thousands in vet's bills.'

'Let's look at some more profit charts.' Sedna flew off to fetch me a new chalk, while Britney arranged herself comfortably. By the time Sedna returned she was snoring, her hooves and nostrils twitching as she did whatever yaks do while they are dreaming. 'Try this one. The question is *Will I make a profit?*'

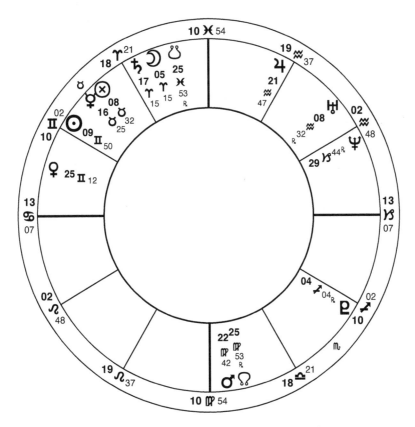

Will I profit? May 31st 1997, 7.15 am BST, London.

He began in the methodical way that is the sure basis of sound astrological judgement. 'Lord 8 is Saturn. For the querent we have Lord 1, which is the Moon, and Lord 2, the Sun. We would give the querent the Moon anyway, but he already has it.'

'Yes. So can we join one of the querent's planets to Saturn?'

'The Moon goes to conjunct Saturn.'

'Yes. But?'

He thought for a moment. 'But it makes a sextile to the Sun first. That could be a prohibition.'

'Yes. But? Bearing in mind that the Moon/Saturn contact will be a conjunction.'

'But an aspect will often fail to prohibit a conjunction.'[42]

'Yes. The prohibition is especially unlikely here because the prohibiting planet is Lord 2. It could still prohibit. For example, the querent's finances might be in such bad condition that he cannot place the bet. That would make sense out of the prohibition. But otherwise, we can assume that the querent and his money are pulling in the same direction. Look again at these three planets, though. What is the Moon doing to the other two?'

'It applies first to sextile the Sun and then to conjunct Saturn. Oh, Master, it's translating light between them! It's carrying the light of the Sun, which is our querent's bank balance, to Saturn, which is the loot.'

'Well spotted my boy. So the querent wins. A lot?'

'I must consider the condition of Lord 8, Master. It's in its fall. Accidentally it's OK, but essentially very weak. The winnings will be small.'

'Yes. Though if we remember the reality of the situation, the punters' profit being something rarely existent outside the world of the imagination, even a small win in the real world is not to be sneezed at.'

'Can we do another, Master?' he asked, bubbling over with eagerness.

'Of course.' I rubbed gently at the chalk marks so as not to wake the sleeper and drew a new chart on her back. 'Same question: *Will I profit?*'

---

[42] For further explanation, see *The Horary Textbook*, pp. 95-97.

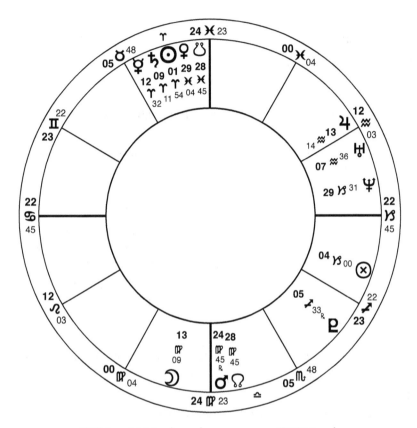

Will I profit? March 22nd 1997, 11.40 am GMT, London.

'Lord 8 is Saturn again. In its fall again. So whatever happens, our querent won't get rich today.'

'Good.'

'For our querent we have the Moon, which is Lord 1, and the Sun, Lord 2.'

'Yes. Is there an aspect?'

'That's easy, Master. Yes, Lord 2 applies to conjunct Lord 8. Querent wins. Lord 8 in its fall again, so again, not much.'

'Good.'

He scratched his head, at which Sedna hopped from my shoulder to feast on the small creatures deposited on the ground. I could see he was thinking. 'But Master, Lord 8 is combust. Surely that means the bookie's money is destroyed, so even if our querent wins there will be no pay-out.'

'You're right in that Saturn is combust. But sometimes we must turn a blind eye to combustion.' Sedna stopped eating, convulsed with ravenical laughter at this inadvertent astrological pun. 'When the Sun is the planet which we wish to connect with the combust planet, we must ignore the combustion, otherwise we would never be able to get anything conjuncted with the Sun. In fact, here it is even a positive sign, because the bookie's money is overwhelmed by the attractive force of our querent's money. But Saturn is in its fall, so still there will be no big pay-out.'

He pulled his antiscion from the hiding place it had found beneath Britney's neck. 'Master,' he began, stroking the furry thing's ear, 'I see that the Sun is on the North Node by antiscion. That must be fortunate for the querent's pocket.'

I clasped him to me in delight, releasing him when strangled coughing from the antiscion he held in his arms told me the poor creature was being squashed in our embrace. 'Yes, my boy. Lord 2 on the North Node favours the querent's pocket. If nothing else were happening in the chart it is possible that this alone could give us a Yes, albeit a cautious one. Here, even though other things give us our main judgement, it is significant. It's a plus for the querent's pocket, so it does a lot to outweigh the limiting testimony of Lord 8 being in its fall.'

'So the win won't be too paltry after all.'

'Quite. We still have the testimony of Saturn in its fall, which we cannot wipe out. But this weighs against it. Not a great win, but not too bad.'

'Master, Lord 2 in its exaltation must mean our querent is rich.'

I thought about correcting him, but by this stage in his tuition my mere glance towards the stick was enough to make my point perfectly clear. This was good, because I was running short of sticks and his Mastercard was at the end of its credit limit. 'Did anyone ask you how much money the querent has?'

He looked suitably abashed. 'No, Master.'

'Then don't answer that question! It is a rule in all astrology:

STICK TO THE POINT

What concerns us here is the amount he will win. Unless Lord 2 is proving a problem to the winning, for instance by being weak and prohibiting the desired aspect, we don't need to concern ourselves with its condition. We can assume the querent knows how much money he has.'

Sedna whispered – as much as a raven can whisper – in my ear. 'Yes, you're right,' I told him. 'In some circumstances the strength of Lord 2 can be important. In those card games where the player with most money has an advantage. If that were the situation here, Lord 2 in its exaltation, combusting the ruler of both the 7th and 8th house would be a strong positive. Say I'm the querent. The exaltation of my money means it looks better than it is. Though it is still strong. Very good for a game of bluff.'

'And your enemy, Lord 7, exalts your money...'

'...which is exaggerated. My enemy has bought into my bluff.'

'Oh, Master, that's so cool,' he giggled. Till Sedna pecked at his head to restore him to a state of decorum. He fluttered up onto my shoulder and I stroked him in approval.

'Look at this one,' I continued, drawing another chart on sleeping Britney's coat. 'Same question: *Will I profit?*'

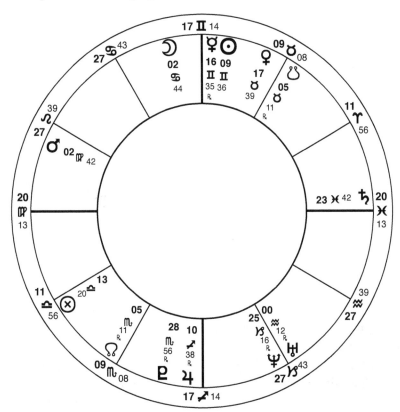

Will I profit? May 31st 1995, 1.31 pm BST, London.

'Moon separates from Mars,' he began, so I reined him in.

'Leaping into charts like that might come in a few years' time. Till then, work through them methodically. Fail to do that and the leaping into charts will never come. Where do we start?'

'We must choose our significators, Master,' he answered, with the air of strained resignation of a schoolboy whose football practice has been cancelled to be replaced with extra maths. 'Lords 1 and 2, Mercury and Venus, are for our querent. Lord 8, Mars, is the money we hope to win. The Moon is also for our querent.'

'Yes. Now you can start trying to join them together.'

'The Moon is separating from its sextile to Mars, Master. That's no use to us. Mars and Venus behold each other...'

'By which you mean what?' I interrupted.

'They are in signs which are in aspect to each other. Virgo and Taurus are in trine, so any planets in Virgo and Taurus behold each other.'

'Just checking. Carry on.'

'But Venus moves faster than Mars. There are occasions when Mars can catch it, when Venus is moving exceptionally slowly, but Mars will never make up 15 degrees on Venus.'

'Maybe Venus will turn retrograde and go back to meet Mars?'

His expression said 'you can't catch me out that easily'. 'Venus is behind the Sun in the order of the signs. It cannot possibly turn retrograde. It does that only when in front of the Sun.' I would have to find some harder questions for him.

'What about Mercury?' I continued.

'Mercury is retrograde, so it will make its aspect to Mars.'

'But?'

'But before it does that it will conjunct the Sun and oppose Jupiter. Either of these would act as a prohibition, preventing its aspect to Mars.'

'So we have no aspect. Our querent cannot win.'

'I haven't checked for translation and collection of light yet, Master.' I was growing increasingly pleased with the lad. 'The Moon separates from Mars and applies to Venus. There is no prohibiting aspect, so this is a translation of light. Our querent wins.'

Ha! I had him. 'No. The querent loses. What do you think shows that?'

He scratched his chin for a while, deep in thought. So intensely did his eyes bore into the chart in their search for inspiration I was surprised he didn't wake Britney. Though it took a lot to wake Britney. 'Venus is in the detriment of Mars,' he ventured.

'Good!

RECEPTIONS ARE IMPORTANT TOO

It's easy to over-use them in charts like this. In boy-girl charts, for instance, we are often concerned mainly with the protagonists' attitudes to each other. There, receptions are of crucial importance. In a chart like this, however, there is no point in trying to analyse the attitudes of all the characters. Especially not those of the bookie's money! In most profit horaries, it is enough to give the receptions a quick glance before ignoring them. Here, a quick glance shows that the receptions are particularly horrible. Mars is in the fall of Venus. Venus is in the detriment of Mars. To add to the mix, the Moon, the connecting planet, is in the fall of Mars. This is a horrible combination.'

'And Mars is weak.'

'Yes. It's peregrine and in the 12th house. There is little money in prospect anyway – even with the best of outcomes. Combine that with this horrible reception and we see there is none at all. The querent loses.'

'These charts aren't always so simple, Master.'

'If they were, Britney would be a great astrologer. And if they were, where would the fun be? We are wrestling with that giant, made of fogs and shadow, that conceals the inner workings of the cosmos. He is a worthy opponent. Sometimes we may gain a fall with scarce effort. Sometimes it takes every ounce of strength we have. And sometimes he defeats us, for all our experience and valour. Look also at the Lord of the Ascendant.'

'Mercury. Oh, it's combust! But it's combust in its own sign. I thought that wasn't an affliction.'[43]

'Combustion in a planet's major dignities is, even at worst, not the devastating thing that combustion otherwise is. It usually works much like a mutual reception between that planet and the Sun. But although it's not so debilitating, it does still carry the idea of not being able to see or be seen. Because of that, we still don't want to see Lord 1 combust, even in its own sign. It shows that the querent can't see. As a general rule, it is strong testimony that the querent's proposed course of action is unwise. In this case, placing the bet is unwise.'

'Gird yourself, here comes another. *Will I profit by placing this bet?*'

---

[43] See *The Horary Textbook*, p. 60.

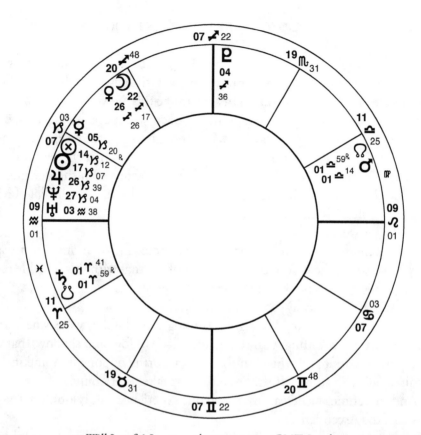

Will I profit? January 7th 1997, 9.15 am GMT, London.

He had learned his lesson, and began methodically. 'The querent has Saturn, Mars and the Moon. The bookie's money is Venus. The Moon goes straight to Venus: the querent wins! At least, this is one strong testimony for the querent winning.' He had indeed learned his lesson.

'What else is happening between our significators?'

'Mars applies immediately to Saturn by opposition. But that is Lord 2, the querent's money, applying to Lord 1, the querent. That can't give us a win: the querent doesn't want his own money back. Even if he did, the aspect is an opposition, so he won't be happy about it. This is a puzzle, Master. What happened?'

'This bet was on a football match. The game was called off because of bad weather. All bets were returned.'

'So our querent's money came back to him. But with regret, as this was not the desired outcome, merely some wasted effort.'

I judged Britney would sleep for a while yet, so drew another chart on her coat. 'It's the same question: *Will I profit?*'

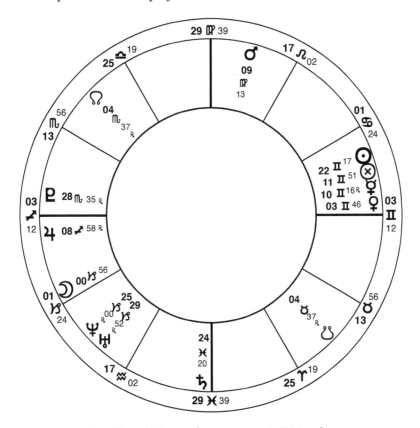

Will I profit? June 13th 1995, 7.33 pm BST, London.

He readied himself for the fray. 'The querent gets Jupiter and Saturn, which are Lords 1 and 2. The money is Lord 8, which is the Moon. That means we can't use the Moon as cosignificator of the querent in this chart, because it has a more important job, signifying the thing asked about.'

'Good. Any aspects?'

'No. The Moon makes no aspect to Jupiter. It will eventually sextile Saturn, but that is prohibited by its previous aspect to Mars. What about the Moon's imme-diate application to the 2nd cusp? I don't suppose that will give a Yes, will it?'

'You don't suppose correctly, boy. If the question were different, perhaps *When will the cheque arrive?* this application might be useful. If the Moon signified the cheque and we knew that the cheque would arrive, either from what we were told or from other evidence in the chart, we could use the Moon's application to the cusp for the timing. It can give us the *when* of a question, but it will not give us the *if.*'

'And here, all that concerns us is that *if.* So this isn't testimony for the querent winning.'

'Exactly.'

'That was simple enough, Master. Can we do another?'

'One more, then. After that it will be time for you to hew wood and draw water. Besides, Britney will be wanting her tea.' Sedna had already nodded off. A bright enough creature, but quite lacking the attention-span needed for the study of astrology. 'Once more: *Will I profit?*'

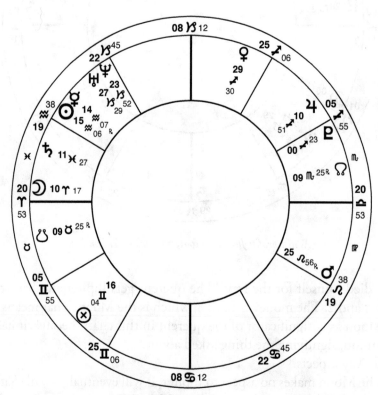

Will I profit? February 4th 1995, 9.40 am GMT, London.

'The querent has Mars, Mercury and the Moon. The money is shown by Jupiter. Oh, Master, it's a lovely strong Jupiter. If there is a win, it will be a big one!'

'Will there be a win? Do we have any aspects?'

'Yes, yes, Master! The Moon makes an immediate trine to Jupiter. And there's another: Mercury is applying to sextile Jupiter.'

'Are you sure about that one?'

'I must give it some thought, Master. The Moon/Jupiter is plain enough. This one....hmm. Mercury is combust. If Mercury were Lord 1, that would be a big problem.'

'Yes, Lord 1 combust is generally a testimony of "don't do it!" But here, it is Lord 2 that is combust. What do you make of that?'

'Combustion is destructive. It might show that the querent doesn't have enough money to place the bet.'

'Very good! That is indeed possible – though we can leave the querent to decide that for himself: it isn't something we need to include in our judgement.'

'No, Master?'

'No! Our job is not to nanny the querent. If he doesn't place the bet, for whatever reason, of course he won't win. The judgement assumes that the bet is made. What about Jupiter's application to Saturn?'

He peered at me worriedly, trying to read my mind. After a moment or two, he must have found the page he was looking for, as his fingers went to his forehead, where through the grime they traced the outline of the branding I had given him. 'I must check my ephemeris, Master.'

'Good! You have saved yourself a beating.' I prodded Sedna into wakefulness with the end my stick. He glanced at the chart, flicked through his memory and squawked, 'Mercury first, Mercury first.'

'With practice you'll be able to see things like this without troubling Sedna. Mercury is so close to the Sun it must be moving fast. It will cover the three degrees or so back to Jupiter quicker than Jupiter, even if it were at its very fastest, could cover the half degree to Saturn. Anyway, even if the Mercury/Jupiter aspect were prohibited, we would still have the clear testimony of Moon to Jupiter. Querent wins and wins big. Now, off to your chores.'

He wandered away, the speed of his going suggesting either an aversion to physical labour or a mind ruminating on what he had learned. Or perhaps both. Britney rose drowsily to her feet, shaking a leg that had gone numb from the weight of her body. With Sedna hopping along behind we made our way back to the cave, they for refreshment, me to close my eyes in contemplation of the harmony of the celestial spheres.

I was awakened by something gnawing at my ear. Before I opened my eyes, my hand closed around something small and furry. The foolish boy had let one of the antiscia out of their hutch whilst feeding them. I kissed its nose and put it back where it belonged.

My temper was quickly soothed by what I saw at the mouth of the cave: a hearty fire burning, the cooking-pot bubbling away and the lad, with Sedna's close advice, preparing our evening repast. It was not long before the meal was ready. Just time enough for a draught of the local brew of fermented yaks' milk that I had picked up while at the village fair the day before. A trifle robust on the nose and lively on the palate, but it did the job.

Over dinner he asked, 'So, Master, if my aim is to make money, I don't need to bother finding the winner, do I? Either by using astrology or by studying form. I can simply ask question after question, *Will I make a profit today?*'

Had he been raiding my kvass supply? 'No, my boy, you cannot. Do not insult Astrology by treating her as a coin-in-the-slot machine. Horary cannot be used mechanically – I've told you that before.'

'Yes, Master,' he confessed, gloomily.

'We can no more do that than we can ask *Will number 1 come up in the lottery? Will number 2?* until we have filled our ticket. If you want results from this, it is necessary to do some work. Get a Yes to *Will I win today?* and then stick a pin in the race-card expecting success, and you will likely be disappointed. A little effort towards identifying the bet is required.'

'I understand, Master. But if I'm casting a profit horary, this is all there is to it: Lord 8 connecting with Lord 1, Lord 2 or the Moon?'

'With those qualifications we've discussed, yes, that is pretty much it. There are a few refinements beyond that, but they are minor. I've told you that astrology is like learning a language. You've now learned the main conjugations. But there are a few irregular verbs with rules of their own. Not that you really need to know them for the subject in hand.'

'Why not, Master? Shouldn't we strive for knowledge?'

'Of course. My point is simply that the practical purpose behind these horary questions can be satisfied by what we've already covered. Be patient a moment, and I will show you some other ways of finding a Yes in the chart. But first consider: while there are other ways of showing a Yes, the wiser course will be to refrain from making the bet unless there is a clear win shown by the main significators. The usual alternatives in betting are winning and losing. If we can shift this to a choice of winning or doing nothing, we have succeeded. Even if we miss the occasional win.'

'But I want to be perfect, Master!'

'So young, my boy.' Britney nodded with the sagacity of experience. 'That's a fine aspiration, but one doomed to be frustrated. There will always be a few charts that are beyond you. Thank goodness! Heaven forbid that astrologers should be infallible. Even when you've learned the conjugations and learned the irregular verbs, in any language you'll find idiosyncratic quirks, odd variants localised in time or place – examples of the glorious abundant complexity that is creation. That this is so is a thing of beauty; let us not mourn because the world cannot all be reduced to simple formulae, readable by our small understandings.'

He had been patient enough, so I beckoned to Britney, asking her if she would mind obliging us further. She muttered something about 'overtime', a word that seems to have been taken directly from English into Yakkish, but lumbered over nonetheless and settled down by my side. I drew a new chart on her coat. 'Once again, *Will I profit?*'

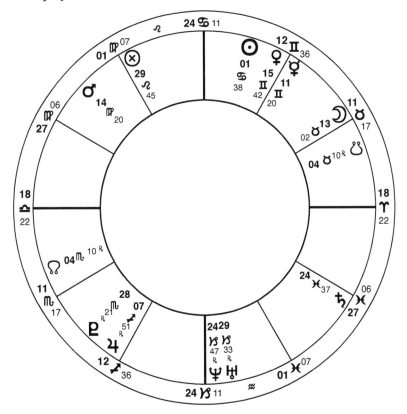

Will I profit? June 23rd 1995, 2.40 pm BST, London.

'The querent has Venus, which is Lord 1, Mars, which is Lord 2, and the Moon. Lord 8 is...oh, Master, it is Venus. What do I do now?'

'Find another significator for the money.'

THE MOON CAN STAND FOR THE PROFIT.
IF LORD 8 IS BUSY, USE THE RULER OF THE NEXT SIGN ROUND.

Using the Moon like this is similar to what we would do in a lost object horary, where the Moon can signify either the querent or the object, and sometimes both, at different stages in the judgement.'[44]

'The next sign round from the 8th cusp is Gemini, so I can use Mercury instead of Lord 8. Mercury goes to square Mars. Querent wins!'

'Although the Moon gets to Mars first. Do you think this is a prohibition?'

'Probably not, Master, because you've just told me I can use the Moon to stand for the profit. So the Moon to Mars shows a win, not a prohibition of the win. And both the Moon and Mercury are strong: it will be a good win.'

'Yes. We are especially encouraged to use the Moon here – although both options are valid – because it is so close to the 8th cusp. It's a common error in horary to think that a planet in a house signifies the things of that house. But there is an occasion when this can be done: this is when, as here, the house-ruler is already is use and the planet which is in that house is very close to the cusp. Then it is sound to rope it in as significator.

'Here's another. *Will I profit?*'

'The querent gets Mercury, Venus and the Moon. Or *maybe* the Moon, perhaps I should say. Lord 8 is Mars. Mars is just inside the 1st house. That must be a good sign.'

'Yes. It's not conclusive, but it's certainly encouraging. We'd still like to see an aspect.'

'Mercury goes to trine Mars. Querent wins.'

'But? Look at that aspect again. What happens?'

'Oh, I see what you mean. Mercury squares Jupiter before it gets to Mars. That's a prohibition.'

'Yes. But what else is happening here?'

'Moon goes straight to Mercury. I can use the Moon to stand for the money. So the querent wins! And the Moon is strong, so he'll win lots.'

'The querent wins, yes. We have other things to consider when assessing the

[44] *The Horary Textbook*, pp. 147-148.

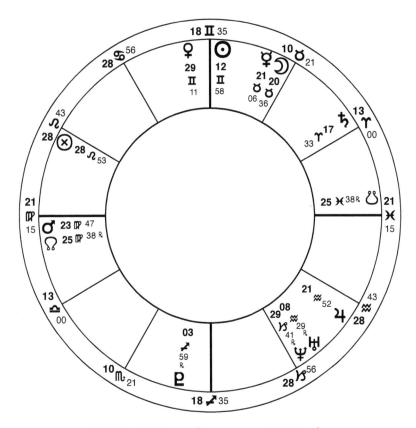

Will I profit? June 3rd 1997, 1.23 pm BST, London.

amount, though. Mars, which is main significator of the money, is peregrine, while there is a major affliction to the 8th house: a badly debilitated Saturn is there. Weighing the Moon's strength too, the win will be OK, but nothing marvellous.'

'Could we have used Saturn to stand for the money here, if Lord 8 were already busy?'

'No. Saturn is over four degrees from the cusp. That's too far. Limit this idea of using a planet on the cusp as substitute to one within, say, two degrees of that cusp.'

Britney's grumbling was growing louder and its phrasing more colourful. To calm her, I announced that this would be the evening's final chart. 'Same question: *Will I profit?*'

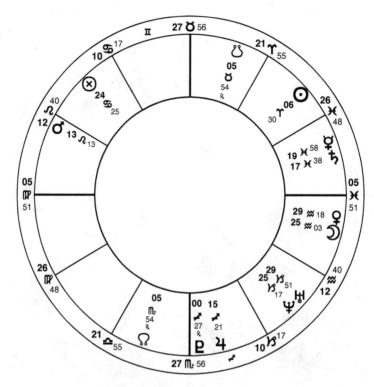

Will I profit? March 27th 1995, 4.25 pm BST, London.

'There is the same sign on the 1st and 2nd cusps, Master. Do I use the ruler of the next sign round for Lord 2?'

'Good thinking, my boy. Yes, you can bring in Venus, ruler of Libra, as Lord 2.'

'What about Mars for Lord 8?'

'This is not such a necessity, because the bookie himself – Lord 7 – is only a shadowy figure at the side of the stage. He isn't involved in the action. But nonetheless, he is on the stage. If the chart urges it upon you, bring in the ruler of the next sign as significator of the money. Here, though, Mars is doing nothing of interest.'

'So if I can use Venus as Lord 2 and the Moon for the money, the Moon applying to conjunct Venus gives us a win.'

'And so it proved. Well done. But now our dear Britney has had quite enough, and it's time you were asleep. Go clean out the antiscia-hutch, then off to your bed. And take these with you,' I added, holding out a handful of palm leaves with charts drawn on them. The question is the same for each of these charts: *Will I make a profit?* You'll find the judgements in Appendix 4.'

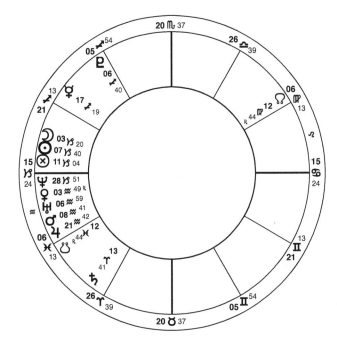

Test chart 13. December 29th
1997, 8.42 am GMT,
London.

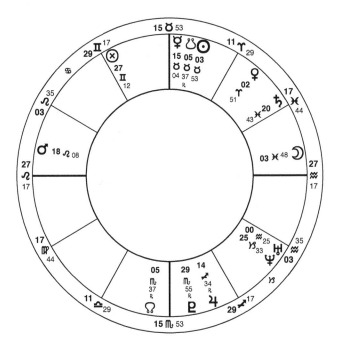

Test chart 14. April 24th
1995, 1.46 pm BST, London.

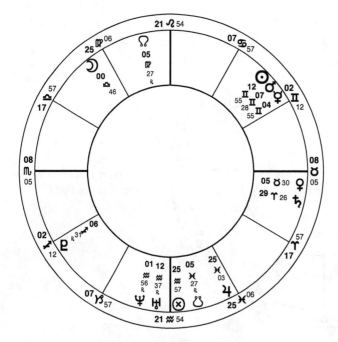

Test chart 15. June 3rd 1998,
5.50 pm BST, London.

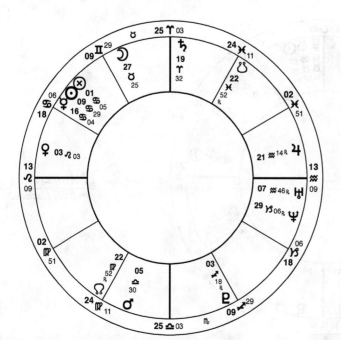

Test chart 16. July 1st 1997,
7.56 am BST, London.

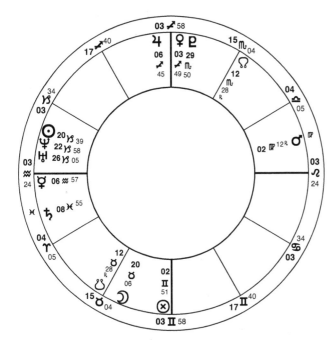

Test chart 17. January 11th 1995, 8.47 am GMT, London.

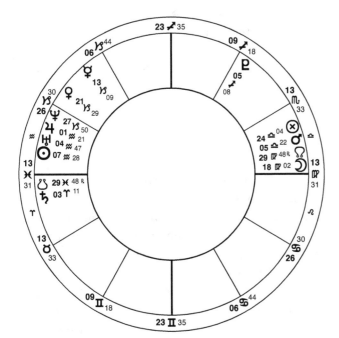

Test chart 18. January 27th 1997, 9.06 am GMT, London.

He scurried away, while I sat stroking Britney's ear in an attempt to console her. After a while, her tongue snaked out to lick my cheek. One brief lick hardly amounted to forgiveness, but I could see she was making an effort.

'His time here is almost done,' I whispered to her, 'and with it your labours. He has learned enough to leave us. No teacher for him now save Astrology itself. Tomorrow he will go. I shall not need to call on you before he leaves.' This time the lick was warm and fervent, caressing my face wetly from ear to ear. Sedna fluttered from beside the dying fire to my shoulder, where he pecked something from my hair. We sat together, watching the embers, while we wondered what would become of the lad when he went on his way.

So why aren't you rich, then?

Over our scant breakfast next day he broke the morning stillness to ask, timidly, 'Master, if you can predict the outcome of these events, why aren't you rich?'

I stood up and swept my arm around me, guiding his eyes across the mountain vistas. 'Rich, my boy? I am the richest man in all the world.' I could see he was touched by the grandeur that lay apparently at his feet, so elevated was our vantage-point. Sorry, too, I knew, to be leaving it. But he would return one day, finding a cave of his own among these dizzying peaks.

'That question,' I continued, 'is the stock response of those who do not wish to entertain the notion that these methods might work. In the same way as *So why haven't you predicted the lottery numbers?* is of those who would thoughtlessly dismiss astrology as a whole. It seems at first a reasonable argument. Consider Sepharial, for instance, who produced "keys" for winning at the race-course, yet died in poverty. Surely this proves his keys were useless? Not at all. They are indeed useless, but their author's poverty does not prove this. I have no interest in betting. I've never understood where the fun lies.'

'But Master,' he interrupted, 'some would say fun isn't necessary. You could earn a good living – if these methods worked.'

'Perhaps. But this is not easy money. The muse of astrology favours only those who dedicate themselves to her. While these techniques may be explained in a few pages, their mastery demands persistent practice over extended periods of time. This is not something to which I choose to devote my working life. This is why I am teaching you: here are the methods, now you go and do the work!

'Above all, there is the question of focus. This is where the fun comes in – or, if you think fun isn't the right word, where an interest in the subject for itself is important. This puzzles those whose main interest is in the money, but, I have found, makes perfect sense to those whose main interest is in the sport. I was discussing this very question with a regular client who had been a tennis champion. She told me the secret of winning at tennis is to remain totally focussed on hitting the ball. The moment the focus shifts to winning that point, winning that game or – Heaven forbid! – lifting the trophy, you are lost. So it is with astrology. I invariably found that as soon as my interest moved from exploring the techniques to making a quick buck, my ability to predict vanished. Focus on the astrology and you might get some money too; focus on the money and you will get nothing.'

'Focus. That makes sense, Master.'

'You're young, boy. I'm sure you can enjoy what money will give you. But devote yourself to Urania and she will give you richer gifts by far. There are places where the caravan rests on its way to her palace. Foolish he who loves the resting-place so much he builds his house there and does not journey on.'

'But where is her palace, Master? Where is this destination? Oh, I want to reach it so much!'

'Ha, my boy, there is no destination! Or none that Urania can provide. Her palace is a mirage that shifts ever away as we venture on. Urania does not dwell in that phantom palace, though. Search hard the caravan in which you travel and you will find her there with you. We journey with her, not to her. This is a lifelong relationship. Perhaps, when you return to your country, you will one day enter a lifelong relationship with a woman. Will there be a destination for that? If you complete, say – and may God grant it you – fifty years of wedded bliss, have you reached the end? Achieved some external goal, so you can tick that off and say you've done it? No. There is no destination. It is the changing of yourself and all else that those fifty years will give you – the voyage itself – that is the destination. So it is with Urania. It is your relationship with her that can give you true gold. To grab the money? Let me tell you a story, my boy:

'There was once a princess of Arabia. She was beautiful as the desert night, generous as a rain-cloud that pours out its whole self to bless the parched earth, richer by far than any fabled queen of which you've ever heard. One day, as she was gazing from her palace window, her eyes chanced upon a young lad, about your age, plying his trade of pickpocket amid the crowds of the bazaar. She saw his nimble fingers dip here, dip there, never resurfacing without a prize. The princess snapped her fingers. Fast as thought, the captain of the guard appeared at her side. She pointed out the thief, and moments later watched as he was lifted from his feet and brought within the palace.

'The guards threw him down on the floor before her. The executioner twitched, in expectation of employ. But no. The lad looked up into her eyes, and the moment he did so she was no longer a princess, but his slave. She dismissed the guard, begged the lad to marry her. Of course, he instantly agreed.

'He was robed in the finest silks as the wedding was prepared. In their separate apartments he dreamed of her beauty, she dreamed of showering him with all the riches her kingdom possessed. Yet on their wedding night, when his lips had scarce touched the chalice of that beauty, the moonlight through the window struck her bracelet lying upon a small table in their nuptial chamber. Green of emerald, deep red of ruby, the cold fierce fire of diamond winked and sparkled in the night. He had the most beautiful of women waiting, eyes closed, in the marital bed – yet his eyes were taken by the sparkling of these jewels. His heart soon followed. With a brief kiss of farewell upon her brow he snatched the bracelet, stuffed it into his pocket, clambered through the chamber window and rode off into the night.

'Next morning, the princess, on whom at birth benevolent spirits had bestowed only happiness, awoke with a better, devoted husband by her side, on whom she poured all her wealth and beauty. The boy, dry with thirst after his frantic escape, staggered into a roadside tavern. Flushed with his new riches, he ordered champagne. So rare was this request in that highway inn that the landlord asked to see his money. The boy reached into his pocket, and found there nothing but the dry sprig of a vine, whose grapes, withered for lack of care, dissolved to dust before his eyes.'

Britney, Sedna and the lad sat in silence as the picture slowly faded from their minds. 'I will heed your warning, Master,' he promised. 'That princess will find me a fine husband! I'll not be distracted by some gaudy jewel.'

'See that you're not, my boy.'

He rose to his feet. It was time for him to leave. He bent forward and kissed Britney on the forehead, a sign either of great affection or of the most foolish bravery. Sedna hopped into the cave to retrieve the boy's credit-card, now pale with wear. A ferocious glare persuaded the lad that a quick ruffling of his feathers would fully suffice for farewell to him.

Next the boy turned awkwardly to me. 'You see this stick, my son?' I asked him. He took it reverently from my hands, for it was a very fine stick indeed. He read aloud the maker's mark: '*Gabbitas and Thring, Purveyors of Fine Beatings to the Gentry*'.

'Admire its craftsmanship. Streamlined, laser-guided. Made from carbon fibre with tungsten bearings: light and flexible, yet firm enough to force understanding into the dullest of brains.' He turned it over in his hands. 'Take it with you, my son. I am old, and one day you will have students of your own. Use it well.'

Tears rose to his eyes, quivering on the brink of falling, like a diver who has climbed higher than his courage can sustain. 'Go now, my boy,' I told him, to spare him embarrassment. My finger went to my lips as he began to speak. 'Go. You will do well.'

He shouldered his new stick, threw his saddle-bags across his rosinante, mounted her, and without a backward glance set off towards the twenty-first century. With Sedna on my shoulder and Britney already asleep by my side, I watched him as he wound his way down the mountain-side. As he was on the point of disappearing, I called after him, my voice picked up by echo upon echo until it sounded like the Hallelujah Chorus ringing among the mountain peaks:

PRACTICE
PRACTICE
PRACTICE
PRACTICE
PRACTICE
PRACTICE
PRACTICE

How to calculate Antiscia

Imagine a line drawn between the solstice points (0 Capricorn and 0 Cancer). Imagine that this line is a mirror. The antiscion of any degree, and of anything in that degree, is its position seen in that mirror. So if something is 2 degrees on one side of this line (at 2 Cancer, say: 2 degrees forward from 0 Cancer) its antiscion will be at 2 degrees on the other side of that line (28 Gemini: 2 degrees back from 0 Cancer).

This reflection around the solstice points shows that the idea is grounded in reality – it was not sucked out of somebody's thumb. There is a direct connection between degrees that are the same distance either side of the solstices. Open your ephemeris at the summer solstice for any year (Sun at 0 Cancer). Pick a number between 1 and 180. Count that number of days forward through the year and note the degree of the Sun on that day. Now count the same number of degrees backwards through the year. The degree of the Sun on that day will be the antiscion of the degree you have just noted. This means that on those two days the time between sunrise and sunset will be exactly the same.

Each sign reflects onto one other sign:

♈	reflects onto	♍
♉		♌
♊		♋
♋		♊
♌		♉
♍		♈
♎		♓
♏		♒
♐		♑
♑		♐
♒		♏
♓		♎

So anything in Aries has its antiscion in Virgo; anything in Taurus has its antiscion in Leo. Learn this table.

Once you know which sign the antiscion of something is in, you need to find its degree in that sign. Original degree + antiscion = 30. The degree the planet is in bodily, added to the degree of its antiscion, will equal 30. So, to find the antiscion, we must take the original degree away from 30. Look back at the example above: if a planet is 2 degrees forward of 0 Cancer, so is bodily at 2 Cancer, its antiscion will be 2 degrees back from 0 Cancer, which is 28 Gemini. 28 + 2 = 30.

Don't worry! However innumerate you may feel you are, this is not complicated. Each sign consists of 30 degrees. Each degree consists of 60 minutes. 60 minutes = 1 degree.

Instead of thinking of each sign as 30 degrees, call it 29 degrees and 60 minutes. It's the same thing (because 60 minutes is the same as 1 degree). But it makes the arithmetic simpler.

Follow this example:

Let's say Mars is at 22.35 Taurus. What is its antiscion?
If Mars is in Taurus, its antiscion must be in Leo (from the table above).
What degree of Leo?
Mars is at 22.35 Taurus.
Take this away from 30 degrees.
But to make it easier, call it 29.60 degrees.

$$\begin{array}{r} 29.60 \\ 22.35 - \\ \hline 7.25 \end{array}$$

So the antiscion of Mars at 22.35 Taurus is 7.25 Leo.
We can check this, because starting degree + antiscion must add up to 30.

$$\begin{array}{r} 7.25 \\ 22.35 + \\ \hline 29.60 \end{array} \text{ which = 30.00}$$

Let's do another one.

What is the antiscion of 14.35 Aries?
From the table above, anything in Aries has its antiscion in Virgo.

What degree of Virgo?
Take 14.35 from 29.60.

$$
\begin{array}{r}
29.60 \\
14.35 - \\
\hline
15.25
\end{array}
$$

So the antiscion of 14.35 Aries is 15.25 Virgo.

The common error here is to end up with starting degree + antiscion = 31 degrees. So, until you get used to this calculation, always check by adding the antiscion you've calculated onto the initial degree to make sure they equal 30. If you follow my suggestion of calling 30 degrees 29.60, you will not make this mistake.

If this seems like hard work, believe me: it isn't. In a very short time you will get used to glancing around the chart to see if the antiscia of any of the significators are doing anything interesting. With a little effort at first you will find that checking antiscia happens almost automatically. You do not have to do the whole calculation. It is enough to think 'Lord 1 is at 19 Gemini. Is there anything around 11 Cancer or Capricorn?' If not – forget it. If there is, then you can calculate the antiscial placement exactly.

How to calculate Arabian Parts

All our degree measurements (6 Aries, 17 Cancer, etc) are measurements of celestial longitude. They tell us how far round the ecliptic a point is. A planet at 12 Taurus is in the second 30-degree chunk of the zodiac (which chunk we call Taurus) and is 12 degrees into that 30-degree chunk.

When we are measuring the distance from one planet to another, counting how many degrees there are between them, we are measuring their distance apart in celestial longitude. But thinking, 'The distance between them is 3 signs and 17 degrees' is clumsy and invites error. It is much easier to work in *absolute longitude*. This is the distance something is from 0 Aries, but is expressed as a number of degrees, not as so many signs and so many degrees. Our example planet at 12 Taurus is at 42 degrees of absolute longitude. To reach it, starting from 0 Aries, we must travel through the 30 degrees that make up Aries, then another 12 degrees of Taurus: 42 degrees in all.

The absolute longitude of 0 degrees of each sign is:

♈	0	♎	180
♉	30	♏	210
♊	60	♐	240
♋	90	♑	270
♌	120	♒	300
♍	150	♓	330

Learn this table.

So a planet at 14 Leo has an absolute longitude of 120 degrees (0 Leo) + 14 degrees = 134 degrees. A planet at 8 Pisces has 330 degrees (0 Pisces) + 8 = 338 degrees.

The business of finding the distance between planet 1 and planet 2, then adding this distance to the Ascendant (or some other point) can be expressed more simply as Asc + planet 2 – planet 1.

Suppose we wish to calculate the position of Fortuna in a chart where the Sun is at 17.34 Leo, the Moon is at 4.52 Libra and the Ascendant is 22.36 Virgo.

The formula for Fortuna is Asc + Moon – Sun.

> **Asc** is 22.36 Virgo.
> > o Virgo is 150 degrees, + 22.36 = 172.36
> **Moon** is at 4.52 Libra.
> > o Libra is 180 degrees, + 4.52 = 184.52
> **Sun** is at 17.34 Leo.
> > o Leo is 120 degrees, + 17.34 = 137.34

> **Asc + Moon:**   172.36
> > 184.52 +
> > ———
> > 356.88

Note the number in the minutes column: 88 minutes. There are only 60 minutes in one degree, but ignore that arithmetical nicety here. If you avoid changing the minutes up into degrees (leaving them here as 88) you ensure that you can take away the third part of the formula without problem. Treat each side of the point as a separate sum, even if you have over 100 in the minute column. This will keep you clear of the usual errors with this calculation.

> **Asc + Moon:**   356.88
> **– Sun:**   137.34 –
> > ———
> > 219.54

So Fortuna is at 219.54° of absolute longitude.
Look at the table of absolute longitudes to find the biggest number that is less than 219.54.
It is 210, which is 0 Scorpio.
So Fortuna is in Scorpio.
Take this 210 away from its absolute longitude of 219.54:

> > 219.54
> > 210.00 –
> > ———
> > 9.54

So Fortuna is at 9.54 Scorpio.

Note: you can add or subtract 360.00 at any time during this calculation if it will make the sum easier. If you find that the number you have to subtract is bigger than the number you got by adding the other two together, add 360 to the number you got from the addition. If the number you end up with when you've finished the sum is bigger than 360, subtract 360 from it. If your final total gives you a number of minutes greater than 60, subtract 60 from it and add 1 to the number of degrees.

Let's do another one. Suppose we want to find the Part of Resignation and Dismissal, the formula for which is Saturn + Jupiter − Sun. Suppose Saturn is at 17.54 Aries, Jupiter at 4.58 Taurus, the Sun at 20.17 Sagittarius.

$$\begin{array}{rl}
\textbf{Saturn + Jupiter:} & 17.54 \\
& \underline{34.58\ +} \\
& 51.112 \quad \text{note the minutes column} \\
& \\
& 51.112 \\
\textbf{- Sun:} & \underline{260.170-} \quad \text{we can't do this, so add 360.00} \\
& \\
& 51.112 \\
& \underline{360.000+} \\
& 411.112 \quad \text{now we can subtract the Sun} \\
& \\
& 411.112 \\
& \underline{260.\ 17\ -} \\
& 151.\ 95
\end{array}$$

So the Part is at 151.95° of absolute longitude.

This is degrees and minutes, though, not degrees and decimals. So now we must adjust the minutes column: 95 minutes = 1 degree and 35 minutes.

So 151.95 = 152.35.

What is the biggest number less than this in the table?

150. So the Part is in Virgo.

$$\begin{array}{r}
152.35 \\
\underline{150.00\ -} \\
2.35
\end{array}$$

So the Part is at 2.35 Virgo.

As a little practice will soon show you, this calculation is far simpler than it might seem. I have had many students professing their innumeracy, but all have learned to do this without too much anguish.

Answers to Set Questions

From page 134:

We want the horse to move fast, so its significator should be *swift in motion*. The significator in station or retrograde would be a strong negative testimony.

From page 158:

1. Lord 1 applies to Lord 8 by square. The existence of an applying aspect between Lord 8 and Lord 1 tells us that the querent will win. We have no information about the condition of Lord 8, so we cannot tell if it will be a big win or a small win. Squares bring the event with difficulty or delay, so there may be some difficulty or delay in getting paid. Usually the context doesn't allow for this, so the fact that the aspect is a square can usually be ignored.

2. Lord 8 applies to Lord 1 by trine. The answer is the same, except that now the aspect is a trine, which gives the event with ease: there will be no difficulty or delay in getting paid. Note that the trine aspect does *not* imply that the win is any bigger.

3. Lord 8 is cazimi and applies to Lord 1 by square. Again, we have an aspect between Lord 8 and Lord 1, so the querent wins. Now we do have information about the condition of Lord 8: it is cazimi. This is extremely strengthening, so it will be a big win (relative to the size of the stake). The aspect is a square, so there may be some delay or difficulty in getting paid, if the context allows this. Note that the square does *not* reduce the amount of the winnings.

4. Lord 2 applies by trine to Lord 8, which is in its fall. We have an applying aspect, this time between Lord 8 and Lord 2, so the querent wins. The aspect is a trine, so there will be no delay or difficulty in getting paid. But Lord 8 is seriously debilitated, so it will be only a small win.

5. The Moon goes to sextile Lord 8, which is on the North Node. The Moon (querent) goes to Lord 8 (the bookie's money) so the querent wins. Lord 8 is on the North Node, which is greatly strengthening, so it will be a big win. The aspect is a sextile, so there will be no delay in payment.

6. Lord 1 applies to oppose Lord 8, which is in its exaltation. The aspect shows the win; the strength of Lord 8 shows it is a big win; but even so, the aspect being an opposition shows that the win isn't worth it in some way. Perhaps I spend all afternoon in the bookmaker's and come home, my pockets stuffed with money, only to find that the Queen chose that afternoon to pay me a surprise visit, so I've missed her.

From page 160:

1. If the ruler of the 8th house is combust, I am sad. Lord 8 signifies the other guy's money. With that so severely afflicted, even if I win the bet he won't be able to pay me. Do not think, 'His money is afflicted, therefore he must lose the bet': it is the money itself that is afflicted, not the money's relationship to him.

2. If the ruler of the 7th house is combust, I am happy. Now it is not the money, but the other guy himself who is afflicted: I win the bet.

APPENDIX 4

Judgements of Set Charts

CHAPTER 1

Test chart 1:

The querent's team has the 1st house, its opponents the 7th.

Mars (Lord 7) is gloriously placed, close to the MC and in its exaltation. Venus (Lord 1) is also in the 10th house, but not only further from the cusp, but also is not in the same sign as the cusp. The enemy must win. And so they did, crushingly.

Test chart 2:

The querent asked whether Sri Lanka would win the Cricket World Cup. As the querent has no partiality towards them, Sri Lanka are given the 7th house.

The Moon (Lord 7) applies to trine Mars (Lord 10), the significator of victory. Yes, Sri Lanka would win. And so it proved.

The reception between the Moon and Mars, each in the other's detriment, is unhelpful. But there is powerful supporting testimony: the Moon is in its exaltation, on an angle, and has lots of light. Even the difficult reception cannot spoil the outcome.

Test chart 3:

England were to play France. The querent supported England.

The Sun (Lord 1) is for England. It is on the South Node. England lose. It would take a lot to outweigh this powerful negative testimony.

Saturn (Lord 7) is in a slightly stronger house than the Sun, which favours the enemy, but exalts the Sun, which favours England more. Neither this, nor the Sun's position near – but not so near – the 7th cusp, is enough to balance out the Sun being on the South Node.

If this were an event chart (as discussed in chapter 2), the Moon's application to oppose Fortuna would be a major testimony. It is not testimony in a horary: do not mix the systems.

France won.

Test chart 4:

Mars (Lord 1) is for the querent's team. It is in a dreadful state: in its detriment and in the unfortunate 6th house. The 6th is the house of Mars' joy, which is a minor positive, but not much of one.

The major positive is that, bad as Mars' position is, it isn't getting any worse. If the team is to go down, its significator must deteriorate in condition. The Sun is in an angular house, which is strengthening, but it is in its fall and is about to set.

Mars is in a cadent (falling) house; the Sun is in its fall: similar testimonies. But Mars is already in that house and the Sun is already in its fall. We are looking for change, not an existing state of affairs.

The Sun is about to set, a literal indication of something going down. It has not yet set, so this is our testimony of change. There is a planet that is about to go down, and it isn't Mars. As only one team will be relegated, that team will not be the one our querent supports. And so it proved.

Test chart 5:

The Sun (Lord 10) is for the champ; Saturn (Lord 4) for the challenger. We could also give the champ the Sun, as natural ruler of kings, but he has it already. We can also give the challenger the Moon, natural ruler of the common people.

Saturn is just inside the 10th house: the challenger is in the champion's power. This alone is almost enough for judgement, but the Moon too is in the 10th house, repeating the testimony. All that is needed now is a quick glance at the Sun to confirm that it isn't in even worse condition, which would be unlikely. The Sun is in the 9th. This is not a strong house, but the Sun is slightly strengthened, because this is the house of its joy. The Sun is not strong, but the challenger's significators are so badly placed it doesn't need to be.

The Moon is void of course, showing there will be no change: the champion will remain champion. The champion won.

Test chart 6:

The Sun (Lord 1) is for the querent's team. By secondary motion – the planet's movement through the zodiac – the Sun is entering the unfortunate 8th house.

This is not a good testimony. By primary motion – the planet's movement across the sky from rising in the east to setting in the west – the Sun is nearing its setting. By this stage of the season, there was no chance of the querent's team being relegated (compare test chart 4), but they will certainly not be going up. Nor did they. Suppose Mars, not the Sun, were Lord 1. Mars is, both essentially and accidentally, the strongest planet in the chart. Being placed right on the IC, the lowest point in the chart, it is about to begin rising towards the Ascendant by primary motion. Were Mars the team's significator, there would be clear testimony of them going up.

CHAPTER 2

Test chart 7:

The Super Bowl. The New England Patriots were favourites to beat the Philadelpia Eagles.
Venus is Lord 10, a significator of the favourites. Its antiscion is at 24.35 Scorpio, just inside the 4th house. This favours the underdogs.
The Moon's first aspect is an opposition to Saturn (Lord 7). This would favour the underdogs, but the Moon makes another aspect. This, the final aspect over its range, is a sextile to the antiscion of Venus (Lord 10). This is testimony for the favourites. The 7 degrees the Moon must travel to oppose Fortuna is too far for consideration in an American football match.
Had it been Lord 1, the Moon or Fortuna inside the 4th house by antiscion, the underdogs might have won. Lord 10 being there is a weaker testimony, and is outweighed by the Moon's final aspect. The favourites win.

Test chart 8:

The West Indies were hot favourites to beat Kenya.
Venus (Lord 7) in the 1st house would be strong testimony for the favourites, but it is too far from the cusp to count.
Mars (Lord 1) is closely combust: strong testimony for the underdogs. Worse still, its antiscion falls at 19.13 Libra, just inside the 7th house. It would need something exceptionally powerful to outweigh these testimonies.
The Moon is on the 4th cusp: strong testimony for the underdog. Its first aspect is to Jupiter, which has no role in this chart and so can be ignored. Its final aspect over its 13-degree range is a square to Venus (Lord 7): further testimony for the underdog.

For good measure, the antiscion of the Sun, which is the dispositor of the Part of Fortune, falls at 20.10 Libra, just inside the 7th house.

Kenya won: a major surprise.

Test chart 9:

Australia were favourites to beat England.

Saturn (Lord 1) is in the 7th house, but much too far from the cusp for this to be significant.

Venus (Lord 4) applies to oppose Fortuna, which favours the underdogs, but is only a minor testimony.

The Moon applies first to trine Venus (Lord 4) and then to square the antiscion of the Sun (Lord 7; 21.20 Capricorn). These testimonies suggest the underdogs may get off to a good start. Its final aspect is a trine to Lord 1 (Saturn). With no other strong testimony, this is conclusive: the favourites win.

England started so well it seemed they could not lose. By the beginning of the final day, the match seemed set for a draw. Australia won. No team batting first in a test match has ever managed to lose after posting so high a score as 551-6 in its first innings.

Test chart 10:

The Champions' League final. Real Madrid were favourites to beat Bayer Leverkusen.

Fortuna on the South Node favours the underdogs, but the main testimonies are given by the Moon. It applies first to conjunct the antiscion of Venus (Lord 7; 5.45 Cancer), then to conjunct the antiscion of Mars (Lord 1; 8.25 Cancer). That is its final aspect, so the favourites win. This being a football match, the Moon is not required to move beyond its 5–6 degree comfort zone, so the first antiscial conjunction is not final.

Predicting the score is at best an educated guess. There is enough testimony to show the losers scoring, but if they score more than once the final score must be at least 3-2. There are probably too few testimonies for that number of goals. The aspect to Mars is within 5 degrees of the Moon's present position, so the game should be decided without extra time. Few goals with at least one goal for the underdogs: 2-1 seems a likely result. This was the last match of the season. Readers of *The Astrologer's Apprentice* were advised to back Real Madrid to win it 2-1 before the season had even begun.[45]

---

[45] *The Astrologer's Apprentice*, issue 20, p. 45.

Test chart 11:

The Worthington Cup final. Manchester United were favourites to beat Liverpool. Venus (Lord 4) sits on the 7th cusp. This isn't the strongest of testimonies, but is worth noting.

The Moon applies to trine the antiscion of Saturn (Lord 7; 7.48 Cancer). It then goes to conjunct the Sun (Lord 1). It must travel 6 degrees to reach the Sun, which could give the favourites victory in extra time. But for the favourites to win in extra time, the match must go to extra time. With two testimonies for the underdogs and nothing for the favourites, it will not: the underdogs will win in normal time.

Not much testimony; nothing at all for the favourites: Liverpool won 2-0.

Test chart 12:

The World Cup final. Brazil were regarded as all but certain to beat France.

There is not much happening here. Mars (Lord 10) approaches the 7th cusp. Had it been closer this would have favoured the favourites, but three and a half degrees of separation is too far for this to count. Venus (Lord 4) has its antiscion at 8.13 Cancer, just inside the 7th house. This is not a major testimony, but with little else in the chart it is significant. The antiscion of Fortuna falls at 12.44 Taurus, just inside the 4th house. This is a powerful testimony: the underdogs must win.

I was perhaps the only TV pundit outside France to predict the French victory.[46] There is no testimony for the favourites, and indeed Brazil failed to score. I was expecting the French to score once, maybe twice. They won 3-0, so my score-line prediction was not correct. The prediction that the favourites would lose in the final was published in *The Astrologer's Apprentice* six months before the tournament began.[47]

CHAPTER 4

Test chart 13:

Lord 1 is Saturn, Lord 2 is Jupiter, Lord 8 is Mercury.

Mercury applies directly to sextile Jupiter: querent wins.

Mercury is in its detriment and in the 12th house (remember the 5-degree rule: a planet within about 5 degrees of the following cusp, and in the same sign as that cusp, is considered to be in that next house), so the winnings will be very small.

---

[46] *Frawley and the Fish,* July 10th, 1998.
[47] Issue 7, pp 16-17.

Test chart 14:

Lord 1 is the Sun, Lord 2 is Mercury, Lord 8 is Jupiter.

Regulus on the Ascendant is a small positive, but does not give a Yes on its own – so as other, conclusive, testimony is necessary it can be ignored.

Mercury and the Sun do not behold Jupiter, so there can be no direct aspect between them (Mercury and the Sun are in Taurus; Jupiter is in Sagittarius: these signs do not aspect each other, so the planets within those signs do not behold each other).

The Moon applies immediately to sextile the Sun and then goes to square Jupiter. The Moon therefore translates light from the Sun to Jupiter, making the desired connection between the two planets: querent wins.

Jupiter is in its own sign and an angular house: a very good win, even if the retrogradation takes a little of the shine off it.

Test chart 15:

Lord 1 is Mars, Lord 2 is Jupiter, Lord 8 is Mercury.

Mercury applies to conjunct Mars. In addition, the Moon will aspect first Mercury and then Mars, translating light between them.

This looks like a clear Yes, but Mars is combust. Except in certain specific circumstances, which are not relevant to profit horaries, no proposed action will turn out well if the querent's main significator is combust. The querent loses.

Test chart 16:

Lord 1 is the Sun, Lord 2 is Mercury, Lord 8 is Jupiter.

The Sun and Mercury are both in Cancer, from where they do not behold Jupiter in Aquarius: there can be no direct aspect between them.

Mercury applies to square Saturn. Jupiter applies to sextile Saturn. Saturn therefore collects the light of Jupiter and Mercury, making the desired connection: querent wins.

Jupiter has dignity only by term, and is retrograde, but it is in an angular house. A win, but nothing to get overly excited about.

Test chart 17:

Saturn is Lord 1, Mars is Lord 2, Venus is Lord 8. Note that even though Pisces is incepted in the 1st house, Jupiter is *not* one of our significators.

Venus and Mars are separating from their aspect, so that is of no interest to us.

Venus applies to square Saturn. This would give a win, but before Venus reaches

Saturn it conjuncts Jupiter. This is a prohibition, preventing the desired aspect. The querent loses.

Test chart 18:

Lord 1 is Jupiter, Lord 2 is Venus, Lord 8 is Mars.

Mars and Venus make no aspect. If you have decided that Mars is separating from Jupiter, go and brand yourself with those magic words: CHECK YOUR EPHEMERIS. Even without the ephemeris, we see that the Sun is near its separating trine to Mars. If Mars is currently direct, this means it must be turning retrograde soon. Mars turns back and makes a trine to Jupiter.

This would give us a Yes, but there is a fly in the ointment. Jupiter makes its sextile to Saturn before it reaches Mars. This is a prohibition, preventing the desired aspect. Mars will then make its own aspect to Saturn, but it is hard to argue that this should be read as a collection of light, because Mars and Jupiter then make their own aspect: Saturn isn't helping here, but is getting in the way.

All is not lost, however: the Moon applies to trine Venus. If it has no other role in the chart, the Moon can be taken to signify the bookie's money, so this gives us a Yes. The querent wins.

Mars is angular, but is in its detriment and opposed by a debilitated Saturn: only a small win.

Index

Only substantive references are listed here

ALSO BY JOHN FRAWLEY
and published by
APPRENTICE BOOKS

THE HORARY TEXTBOOK

Clear and comprehensive, this is the standard modern text for the study of horary astrology. Frawley begins with the claim that horary 'is quick, simple and effective', then spends 250 pages demonstrating exactly that. Forget any ideas of horary being dry, antiquated or rule-bound: this is horary as it lives, straightforward and open to everyone. One of the indispensable books for the twenty-first century astrologer.

HORARY PRACTICE

The companion volume to *The Horary Textbook*. You've learned the techniques – now give those astrological muscles a rigorous workout, as John guides you step by step through a long series of judgements on a huge variety of questions. This is your chance to stand at the elbow of a master astrologer as he works, absorbing the thought processes that will lead you to mastery of the horary craft.

Horary Practice is due for publication in the summer of 2010.

ALSO BY JOHN FRAWLEY
and published by
APPRENTICE BOOKS

THE REAL ASTROLOGY

Winner of the Spica Award for International Book of the Year, *The Real Astrology* provides a searching – and often hilarious – critique of modern astrology and a detailed introduction to the traditional craft. It contains a clear exposition of the cosmological background and a step-by-step guide to method, accessible to those with no prior knowledge of the subject, yet sufficiently thorough to serve as a *vade mecum* for the student or practitioner.

Philosophically rich – genuinely funny – written by a master of the subject and informed with invaluable practical advice. – *The Mountain Astrologer*

Wit, philosophy and a thoroughly remarkable depth of scholarship. I will be ever thankful to John Frawley for this gem of a book. – *AFI Journal*

Required reading for all astrologers – *Prediction*

THE REAL ASTROLOGY APPLIED

This collection of notes and essays handles in greater depth subjects raised in *The Real Astrology*. It elucidates both technical matters and significant points of the philosophy that forms the basis of the practical craft.

An excellent book. Should be read and reread by all who intend calling themselves astrologers. – *Considerations*

Highly readable – a virtual fountain of knowledge and technique – makes some of the most complex astrological material go down like a brandy snifter full of the smoothest amber elixir. – *The Mountain Astrologer*

Printed in the USA
CPSIA information can be obtained
at www.ICGtesting.com
LVHW080908210924
791743LV00012B/1096